Please renew/return this item by the last date shown.

So that your telephone call is charged at local rate,
please call the numbers as set out below:

	From Area codes 01923 or 0208:	From the rest of Herts:
Renewals:	01923 471373	01438 737373
Enquiries:	01923 471333	01438 737333
Minicom:	01923 471599	01438 737599

L32b

THE OLD CUSTOMS AND CEREMONIES OF LONDON

MARGARET BRENTNALL

THE OLD CUSTOMS AND CEREMONIES OF LONDON

B. T. Batsford Ltd

London & Sydney

First published 1975

© Margaret Brentnall 1975

ISBN 0 7134 2933 X

Printed in Great Britain by
Cox and Wyman Limited, Fakenham, Norfolk
for the publishers B. T. Batsford Ltd
4 Fitzhardinge Street, London W1H 0AH
and 23 Cross Street, Brookvale, NSW 2100, Australia

CONTENTS

THE ILLUSTRATIONS

ACKNOWLEDGEMENTS

A book such as this invites a boundless number of acknowledgements, for it would be difficult to embark upon the work at all without the aid of those whose specialized knowledge is far greater than one's own. So I will convey my gratitude section by section.

First of all I want to express my warmest thanks to the Public Relations Department of the Corporation of London, and especially to Miss Christine Davison and Miss Judith Dagworthy for untiring help in checking details and enabling me to attend City ceremonies; also to Miss B. Masters, Deputy Keeper of the Records, for valued advice on points of historic detail. To the Livery Companies my grateful thanks are extended for their courtesy and willing help, and for inviting me to attend the Trial of the Pyx, the Knollys Rose Ceremony, and the Stationers' Cakes and Ale custom.

The Monarchy and the Services – I thank most sincerely Mr Peter A. Wright, Royal Almonry, and Mr C. S. Scull, Serjeant of the Vestry, Chapel Royal, St James's Palace, for enabling me to attend the Royal Maundy Service and the Feast of the Epiphany Service, and for their valuable comments on my text. Grateful thanks for advice are also extended to Colonel John Dymoke, Hereditary Grand Champion. To Mr E. R. Wheeler, Duchy of Lancaster Office, I owe thanks for much information on the Manor of the Savoy; and on the Yeomen of the Guard I am indebted to Sergeant Major Phillips, Queen's Bodyguard, St James's Palace, and to Chief Yeoman Warder C. Taylor of the Tower of London. To the Queen's Bargemaster, Mr H. A. (Bert) Barry, I owe especial thanks for a wealth of information on the Royal Watermen and Doggett's Coat and Badge Race, and the late Mr Harry Phelps was kindness itself in recounting his Doggett memories and lending items from his scrapbooks. My thanks also to Mr Michael Turk, Bargemaster and Swan Marker, Vintners' Company, for enabling me to accompany the Swan Uppers and for information concerning this ancient custom. On the Services – this section would, I feel sure, have included many a blunder without the advice of Major R. A. G. Courage, PRO Household Division, and of Lieutenant Commander Patrick Stearns, Flag Lieutenant to the Admiralty Board, aid for which I am deeply grateful. I am also indebted to the Royal Navy and Royal Air Force PROs, Ministry of Defence; to Lieutenant Commander Thomas P. Heard and Lieutenant Commander Cooper of the Royal Naval College; and to Lieutenant Colonel Patrick Massey of the Honourable Artillery Company. On the Chelsea Pensioners, I wish to express wholehearted thanks to Captain C. Townsend, Captain of Invalids, Royal Hospital, for regaling me so generously from his fount of knowledge.

Parliament – I owe very sincere thanks for advice on many points of detail to Mr Maurice Bond, Clerk of the Records, Palace of Westminster; and to Miss D. M. P. Malley, Crown Office, House of Lords.

The Law – to Mr Quentin Edwards, Bencher of the Middle Temple, I offer my gratitude for his advice and interest, and for introductions to other sources of information; and to the Librarians of the Inns of Court I am grateful for their patient co-operation. To the Headmasters and Archivists of the Schools mentioned, and the Rectors and Vicars concerned with customs described, I offer thanks for their interest and help. To Mr W. T. Cook, Hon. Librarian of the Ancient Society of College Youths, I am indebted for enlightening me on bell-ringing and for enabling me to watch the bell-ringers of St Paul's in action. My thanks, also, to Miss Rankin of the Vic-Wells Association, to Mr John Yeowell of the Sublime Society of Beef Steaks, and to Mrs E. Peel, Warden of the Fern Street Settlement.

MARGARET BRENTNALL

Highgate, London.

The Author and Publishers would like to thank the following for permission to use photographs in this book: The British Tourist Authority (Pls 4, 7, 10, 15); Keystone Press Agency Limited (Pls 2, 3, 5, 16, 21, 22); The Press Association (Pls 9, 11); *The Times* and The Central Press Photos Limited (Pls 6, 12, 13); The Theatre Royal, Drury Lane (Pl. 20); Whitbread & Co. Ltd. (Pl. 1). Plates 8, 14, 17, 18, 19, 23, 24, and 25 are from photographs by the author.

CALENDAR OF CUSTOMS
AND CEREMONIES

Many of these events take place on dates which vary from year to year in order to conform with the diary of the Lord Mayor and of other notabilities who may be attending.

Event	Venue	Date
JANUARY		
Offering of the Queen's Gifts on the Feast of the Epiphany	Chapel Royal, St James's Palace	6 January
The Baddeley Cake (Twelfth Night Cake)	Theatre Royal, Drury Lane	6 January
King Charles I Commemoration Services and wreath-laying ceremonies	Services – usually at St Mary-le-Strand, St Margaret Pattens, and St Martin-in-the-Fields; wreath-laying ceremonies and services beside King Charles I's statue in Trafalgar Square and at the Banqueting House, Whitehall	On and near 30 January
FEBRUARY		
Blessing of the Throats	St Etheldreda's Church, Ely Place	3 February

Event	Venue	Date
Sir John Cass School – Red Feather Day	Church of St Botolph Without Aldgate	On or near 20 February

FEBRUARY/MARCH

Event	Venue	Date
Trial of the Pyx	Goldsmiths' Hall, Foster Lane	In February or March
Pancake Greaze	Westminster School	Shrove Tuesday
Cakes and Ale custom of the Stationers' Company	Stationers' Hall, Ave Maria Lane	Ash Wednesday

MARCH

Event	Venue	Date
Bridewell Service	St Bride's Church, Fleet Street	Second Tuesday in March
Grimaldi Commemoration Service	Holy Trinity Church, Dalston	Usually a Sunday in mid-March
Oranges and Lemons Service	St Clement Danes Church, Strand	Weekday, second half of March

MARCH/APRIL

Event	Venue	Date
Royal Maundy Distribution	Westminster Abbey (when the distribution takes place in London)	Maundy Thursday (the Thursday before Easter)
Butterworth Charity – Distribution of Hot Cross Buns	Priory Church of St Bartholomew-the-Great, West Smithfield	Good Friday, after 11 am Service
Hot Cross Buns at the Widow's Son	Widow's Son Tavern, Devons Road, Bromley-by-Bow	Good Friday (but tavern destined eventually for demolition)

Event	*Venue*	*Date*
APRIL		
Stow Commemoration Service – Changing the Quill Ceremony	Church of St Andrew Undershaft, Leadenhall Street	On or near 5 April
MAY		
Florence Nightingale Commemoration Service	Westminster Abbey	On or near 12 May
Verdict of the Trial of the Pyx and the Pyx Luncheon	Goldsmiths' Hall, Foster Lane	Usually during May
Beating the Bounds, Tower of London	Tower of London	Ascension Day – once in three years
Beating the Bounds, Manor of the Savoy	Queen's Chapel of the Savoy, and tour of boundary marks of the Manor of the Savoy	Ascension Day – approximately once in five years
Commemoration of the murder of King Henry VI	Wakefield Tower, Tower of London	21 May
The Spital Sermon	Church of St Lawrence Jewry, Gresham Street	Mid-May
MAY/JUNE		
Beating Retreat by Household Division and two weeks later by another regiment or arm of the Services	Horse Guards Parade	Late May or early June
Founder's Day of the Chelsea Pensioners	Royal Hospital, Chelsea	On or near 29 May
Pepys Commemoration Service	Church of St Olave, Hart Street	On or near 26 May

Event	*Venue*	*Date*
MAY/JUNE *continued*		
Election Day Procession of the Skinners' Company in which the boys of Christ's Hospital participate	From Skinners' Hall, Dowgate Street, to Church of St Mary Aldermary	Corpus Christi Day
JUNE		
The Queen's Birthday Parade – Trooping the Colour	Horse Guards Parade	A Saturday morning in June
Beating Retreat by the Royal Marines	Horse Guards Parade	In June, every third year, in honour of the birthday on 10 June of their Captain General, the Duke of Edinburgh
Election of Sheriffs	Guildhall	24 June, unless date falls at the week-end
Ceremony of the Knollys Rose	Mansion House	On or near 24 June
'Bubble Sermon' of the Stationers' Company	St Martin-Within-Ludgate	First Tuesday in June
JULY		
Swan Upping	Temple Stairs to Henley	Six days in July (usually mid-July)
Installation Day Procession of the Vintners' Company	Vintners' Hall, Upper Thames Street, to Church of St James Garlickhythe	Usually in second week of July

Event	*Venue*	*Date*
AUGUST		
Doggett's Coat and Badge Race	River Thames, London Bridge to Chelsea	On or near 1 August
SEPTEMBER		
Battle of Britain Sunday	Principal London Services at Westminster Abbey and at the RAF's Church of St Clement Danes in the Strand	A Sunday in mid-September
St Matthew's Day Procession of the Christ's Hospital boys and girls	From Church of St Sepulchre-Without-Newgate, Holborn Viaduct, to the Mansion House	21 September
Admission of Sheriffs	Guildhall	28 September (unless date falls at week-end)
Election of the Lord Mayor	Guildhall	29 September (unless date falls at week-end)
OCTOBER		
Judges' Procession on opening of the new legal year	From Westminster Abbey to Palace of Westminster and at Law Courts	1 October (or first weekday in October if date falls at week-end)
Quit Rent Ceremonies	Royal Courts of Justice, Strand	Usually during second half of October
Costermongers' Harvest Service	Church of St Martin-in-the-Fields	Usually a Sunday in first half of October

15

Event	Venue	Date
OCTOBER *continued*		
Harvest of the Sea Thanksgiving Service	Church of St Mary at Hill, Lovat Lane, Eascheap	Usually a Sunday in first half of October
The Lion Sermon	Church of St Katharine Cree	16 October
Trafalgar Sunday – Commemoration Service of the Battle of Trafalgar	Trafalgar Square	Sunday nearest to anniversary of the Battle of Trafalgar, 21 October
,,	Chapel of the Royal Naval College, Greenwich	Sunday nearest to 21 October
National Service for Seafarers	St Paul's Cathedral	Wednesday nearest to anniversary of Battle of Trafalgar, 21 October
NOVEMBER		
State Opening of Parliament	Palace of Westminster	Usually early in November
Remembrance Sunday – the Cenotaph Ceremony	Whitehall	On or near 11 November
Admission of the Lord Mayor	Guildhall	Second Friday in November
Lord Mayor's Show	Route – Guildhall to Royal Courts of Justice, via the Mansion House where the Lord Mayor takes the Salute	Second Saturday in November
Lord Mayor's Banquet	Guildhall	Monday following Lord Mayor's Show

Calendar of Customs and Ceremonies

Event	Venue	Date
DECEMBER		
Presentation to Chelsea Pensioners of the Australian Cake	Royal Hospital, Chelsea	During month
Chelsea Pensioners' Cheese Ceremony	Royal Hospital, Chelsea	During month

EVENTS WHICH TAKE PLACE REGULARLY DURING THE YEAR:

Event	Venue	Date
Ceremony of the Keys	Tower of London	Nightly
Changing of the Guard	Buckingham Palace, St James's Palace, Horse Guards, Tower of London	Daily
Court of Common Council	Guildhall	Alternate Thursdays – except during Summer and Christmas recesses
Farthing Bundles	Fern Street Settlement, Bromley-by-Bow	Alternate Saturday mornings
Swearing on the Horns	Wrestlers' Inn, Highgate	Twice yearly, usually an evening in Spring and Autumn

CHAPTER ONE

The City

It is inevitable that the City should be the starting point of any book on the customs and ceremonies of London, for this is the oldest part of the capital and the cradle of custom and tradition. The boundaries of this historic area, known as the Square Mile, stretch roughly from Temple Bar to Aldgate and from the north bank of the Thames to City Road, and such place names as Ludgate, Aldgate, and London Wall are reminders of the old encircling walls and gates. In earlier times the City *was* London, the place where Londoners lived as well as worked, and this fact is emphasised when one remembers that Sir Thomas More was born in Milk Street and John Milton in Bread Street, both in the neighbourhood of Old St Paul's. It was the people who dwelt in the closely packed streets of this early City of London who developed the independent spirit which can be detected in so many of the old customs and ceremonies that have survived. There is nothing artificial or 'quaint' about these City customs and traditions. They are part of the history, rights and liberties of the people, and every wind of change that has blown through the City streets, however turbulent, has left them undisturbed.

The 'monarch' of this ancient territory is the Lord Mayor who, within the City, yields precedence only to the Sovereign. His residence is the Mansion House; his Household includes such dignitaries as the Swordbearer, the Common Cryer and Serjeant-at-Arms, the City Marshal – and, in former times, the Common Hunt and the Fool. A curious custom used to exist that, at the Lord Mayor's Banquet, the Fool must leap into the custard as a token of celebration. This meant, literally, that he plunged fully clad into a vast bowl of custard – an episode guaranteed to add greatly to the mirth of the occasion. Whether the custard was eaten afterwards, I am not sure.

This fool's activity was mentioned, rather obscurely, by Ben Jonson (1573–1637) in the following lines:

> *He may, perchance, in tail of a Sheriff's dinner,*
> *Skip with a rime o' the table, from new nothing,*
> *And take his almain leap into a custard,*
> *Shall make my Lady Mayoress and her sisters*
> *Laugh all their hoods over their shoulders.*

The first Mayor of London was Henry FitzAilwyn in *c.* 1192. Prior to this the Portreeve held the title and power of First Officer. Fitz-Ailwyn continued to hold office until his death in 1212. It was King John who, a few months before the sealing of Magna Carta in 1215, granted by Charter the right to elect a Mayor annually. The title Lord Mayor is first recorded in 1414, and is generally regarded as dating from that time although it had been used, in Latin form, during the previous century. The rights and privileges of the citizens of London are of singular antiquity, dating back to Saxon times, and they were recognised by William the Conqueror in his Charter of 1067.

The Court of Common Council, which still meets in Guildhall on alternate Thursdays, evolved during the course of the thirteenth and fourteenth centuries. It is presided over by the Lord Mayor (or in his absence by an Alderman who has previously served as Lord Mayor), and the words with which he opens the proceedings are always the same: '*Domine dirige nos, Amen*' (O Lord guide us, Amen). *Domine dirige nos* is the motto on the City Coat of Arms. The Court is composed of 25 Aldermen in addition to the Lord Mayor and over 130 Common Councilmen, and when summoned there must be at least two Aldermen and 40 Common Councilmen in attendance together with the Lord Mayor or his *locum tenens*. In Parliamentary terms, the Court of Common Council is the City's equivalent to the House of Commons, while the Court of Aldermen can be regarded as the Upper House. There is also the assembly of Liverymen in Common Hall who meet in order to elect the Sheriffs, the Chamberlain and the candidates from whom the new Lord Mayor will be chosen.

For the fortnightly meeting of the Court of Common Council the

Lord Mayor arrives at Guildhall accompanied by his Household Escort – the City Marshal, the Swordbearer, and the Common Cryer and Serjeant-at-Arms; the last-named is the Macebearer, and although the title sounds like two members of the Escort it is a joint office, held by one man. One of the sights which fascinates visitors to London is to encounter this trio, marching to Guildhall from, say, the Corporation's Church of St Lawrence Jewry after a special service attended by the Lord Mayor; bearing the City Sword and Mace, they proceed with measured step, quite oblivious of the City workers who continue unconcerned along the pavements. Few people realise that within the Swordbearer's imposing fur head-dress (known as the Cap of Maintenance) is a concealed pocket which holds the Lord Mayor's key to the City Seal Box. This pocket also used to hold instructions regarding action to be taken should the Lord Mayor collapse and die on any public occasion, but these instructions are now carried in one of the Swordbearer's pockets. The City Marshal, who leads the Escort, is clad in a white-plumed cocked hat and scarlet coatee with gold epaulettes.

The Lord Mayor is nominated, as I have already related, by the Liverymen of the City, who submit the names for final selection by the Court of Aldermen. The candidates must be Aldermen who have served a term of office as Sheriff (although a Sheriff need not necessarily be an Alderman). The Aldermen of the City of London have always differed from those of other cities in being elected for life instead of for a limited span of years – although today there is some limitation, for they cease to hold office on reaching the retirement age of magistrates. The Lord Mayor, on entering upon his term of office, becomes the City's Chief Magistrate. There are 26 Wards in the City of London, of which 25 each have their own Alderman and up to 12 Common Councilmen (the number being governed by the size of the Ward). A senior Alderman, who has served as Lord Mayor, represents the 26th Ward, the Ward of Bridge Without, which has no electors and is a relic of the days when the City exercised jurisdiction in Southwark.

Election of the Lord Mayor takes place on Michaelmas Day (29 September). On this day the reigning Lord Mayor and Sheriffs leave the Mansion House in full state and are received at Guildhall by the Aldermen and Officers in the Livery Hall. They are presented with nosegays of garden flowers by the Keeper of the Guildhall, and throughout the subsequent ceremonies of the morning they retain these posies, a custom dating from the days when sweet-scented flowers and herbs were regarded as protection against the infections and evil smells of the streets. The dais in Guildhall is strewn with aromatic herbs and these are also scattered in the adjacent Livery Hall where the Court of Aldermen is held. Infections and evil smells are mercifully less prevalent today, yet the delightful old custom of the herbs and posies still prevails at many of London's ancient ceremonies.

Before the Election takes place the Lord Mayor and high Officers attend Divine Service in the Church of St Lawrence Jewry – a custom which dates from the Election of Richard Whittington in 1406 and at that time held in the Guildhall Chapel. Afterwards, all walk in procession (still carrying the posies) to Guildhall, where the Liverymen have meanwhile been gathering.

I should mention at this point that Guildhall, throughout Election Day, presents a most unusual appearance, the whole lower frontage being barricaded with a construction known as 'the Wickets'. Behind the doors of each wicket appear the heads and shoulders of the Beadles, mace in hand and looking ready to obstruct any intruder on this great City occasion – which is, of course, the purpose of the Wickets. The names of the Livery Companies appear along the whole length of the Wickets.

The procession makes its way to the Hustings, as the dais is called (a heritage from the ancient Court of Hustings), and then the Common Cryer and Serjeant-at-Arms demands that 'All those who are not Liverymen depart the Hall on pain of imprisonment'.

The Election proceedings are opened by the Common Cryer and Serjeant-at-Arms with the words 'Oyez, Oyez, Oyez. You good members of the Livery of the several Companies of this City summoned to appear here this day for the election of a fit and able person to be Lord Mayor of this City for the year ensuing, draw near and give your attendance. God Save the Queen'.

Before the voting starts the reigning Lord Mayor, together with the Aldermen who have already passed the Chair, the Recorder and the Town Clerk, retire in silent and solemn procession to the Livery Hall. The City Marshal and the Swordbearer lead the way, and the door is closed by the City Marshal, who remains beside it on guard – the whole purpose of this exodus being to ensure that the Livery vote is 'free and unfettered'. In the Livery Hall the Swordbearer lays the City Sword to rest on a bed of rose petals – an act which symbolises that the proceedings are *sub rosa*, in secret. Legend tells that Cupid gave a rose to Harpocrates, the God of Silence – hence the tradition of the rose as a symbol of silence.

The voting, meanwhile, begins in the Great Hall. The names of candidates are read out and displayed, and the Liverymen are told to name two candidates from whom the final choice will be made by the Aldermen. As support for each candidate is requested, the voters raise their hands and shout 'All' when in favour. Voting over, the names are conveyed to the Livery Hall, where a Court of Aldermen is held immediately. The final decision is reached by ballot and, following speeches, the silent procession makes its way once more to the Hustings, the rose petals in the Livery Hall lying crushed where the weight of the City Sword has lain.

The Lord Mayor Elect is now escorted by the Swordbearer to his seat of honour on the left-hand side of the reigning Lord Mayor, and he is then required to declare his assent to take upon himself the office upon 'pain and peril that shall fall thereon'. Needless to say he does so, for he is unlikely to decline the honour at this late hour. His Shrieval Chain is placed upon his shoulders and speeches by the Lord Mayor, the Lord Mayor Elect, and the late Sheriffs bring the ceremony to an end. It is a ceremony which ushers in a year of near-monarchy for the newly-elected citizen shortly to undertake the City of London's most exalted office. But from this day until Admission Day he remains discreetly invisible on official occasions, never competing with the reigning Lord Mayor during the latter's final weeks of power. It is during this period that he attends at the House of Lords to receive the Queen's consent to his election, conveyed by the Lord Chancellor in the Prince's Chamber – a ceremonial occasion for which he wears Court Dress, his Violet Gown and Shrieval Chain.

On Admission Day, the second Friday in November, the new Lord

Mayor is sworn in at Guildhall. But first of all there is a Luncheon at the Mansion House at which the Outgoing Lord Mayor and the Lord Mayor Elect are joint hosts. Then they set out for Guildhall, the former in full dignity while the Lord Mayor Elect emerges unostentatiously by a side door.

At Guildhall the ceremony begins and the new Lord Mayor enters his year of glory. There are no more side doors for him after the symbols of office – the Sword and Mace, the Crystal Sceptre, the Seal and the sixteenth-century City Purse – have been passed to him. All the ancient ceremonial of centuries survives as each symbol of office is carried forward, the bearer offering three low reverences as he approaches and again as he retires. Then comes the moment when the two Lord Mayors, the old and the new, exchange seats – the most impressive moment in all the ritual of election and admission. The procedure of transfer of office is known as the Silent Change, and total silence reigns as the former Lord Mayor yields place to his successor. How does he feel, one wonders, during the deathly quiet of the Silent Change? Does he regret stepping down from so much power and pomp to ordinary citizenship? Or does he sense a lurking relief at the return to normality after so exacting a period of office? The new Lord Mayor's sentiments are much more predictable, for he cannot fail to experience exhilaration at the prospect of the year of honour and responsibility that lies ahead. There is an inflexible tradition in the City that from this moment – or at any rate after the Lord Mayor's Banquet – the retiring Lord Mayor steps into the shadows. The opening period of the reign of the Lord Mayor is never clouded by the proximity of his predecessor.

The next day (the second Saturday in November) heralds in the Lord Mayor's Show. This is when the Lord Mayor is conveyed to the Royal Courts of Justice in his elaborate gilded coach, drawn by a team of six mighty Shires from the stables of the City brewery of Whitbread. (Whitbread have provided the horses for this occasion since 1955). His bodyguard is composed of the Company of Pikemen and Musketeers of the Honourable Artillery Company, and also taking part are Naval, Regimental and Royal Air Force bands, the Household Cavalry and the State Trumpeters. Floats form a large part of the public entertainment of the Lord Mayor's Show – a seemingly endless array of decorated floats devoted to topical subjects and emphasising the Lord Mayor's theme for the year.

The Lord Mayor takes the salute and watches this vast procession from a draped stand on the front of the Mansion House; then, in his gilded coach, he joins the procession at the rear, with the City Marshal, mounted on horseback, preceding him. The Outgoing Lord Mayor, still highly honoured but his star in the descendant, rides in an ungilded State Carriage.

There is ancient tradition behind the ceremonial of Lord Mayor's Day. In 1215 King John proclaimed that the new Mayor must attend upon the Sovereign or, in his absence, upon the Royal Justices to obtain the Royal approval. As time went by the alternative became the rule. From 1215 onwards the Mayor must have travelled in some state, but it was in the sixteenth century that the elements of pageantry developed for which the Lord Mayor's Show is famous. For centuries the destination was Westminster – until the opening in the nineteenth century of the Royal Courts of Justice in the Strand. Here the Lord Mayor makes his statutory declaration of office before the Lord Chief Justice and Judges of the Queen's Bench Division. The procession usually leaves Guildhall at about 11.30 am and proceeds via Cheapside, Ludgate Hill and Fleet Street to the Royal Courts of Justice, returning via the Victoria Embankment to the Mansion House.

Two days later the Lord Mayor's Banquet is held in Guildhall, which has been its location since 1501. The Prime Minister is the Guest of Honour and it has been the tradition for the past 200 years or so for turtle soup to be served. Scarcity, however, has caused an occasional lapse in the turtle soup routine. The scene at the Lord Mayor's Banquet is of exceptional brilliance, with trumpets heralding the approach of the Lord Mayor and distinguished guests, who walk in procession to their seats at the top table to the accompaniment of music from the gallery. The Banquet represents the last phase of glory for the Outgoing Lord Mayor, for although the new Lord Mayor now holds the centre of the stage one of the prime objects of the evening is to pay due honour to his predecessor.

The Lord Mayor's Show, grand sight that it is today, is nothing like so spectacular as it was centuries ago. The City of London was famous for its pageants, not only for Lord Mayor's Day but also for royal receptions. For the latter, elaborately constructed arches were erected at the entry point and along the streets through which the procession would pass. Speeches, poems and songs were prepared by the poets and musicians of the day, and giant figures were a special feature of the celebrations, either carried in the procession or mounted on the reception arch.

This is where the two mythical giants of Guildhall, Gog and Magog, first come into the picture, and they still look down upon all proceedings from their respective heights at the west end of the Great Hall. These wooden Guildhall giants have been particularly susceptible to fire. The present versions were carved by David Evans as replacements for the 1708 giants by Richard Saunders destroyed during the last war. Their names should rightly be Gogmagog and Corineus, for according to legend Gogmagog was a British giant who suffered defeat at the hands of the Trojan Corineus. They long retained their names of Gogmagog and Corineus, but as time went by the first name was divided between them and Corineus was forgotten.

Among the great City pageants and royal receptions the earliest on record was in 1236, when Henry III and his Queen, Eleanor of Provence, were received by the Mayor, Aldermen, and 360 citizens, all mounted and magnificently clad in robes of embroidered silk. Each horseman carried in his hand a cup of gold or silver, representing the status of the Mayor of the City of London as Chief Butler at the coronation of the Sovereign. Especially impressive, too, was the welcome accorded to Henry V in 1415 after his victory at Agincourt. In 1432 Henry VI was received with similar pomp. Giants figured in all these receptions, but it was not until Mary I and Philip of Spain entered the City in 1554 that Gog and Magog made their first appearance – undoubtedly as Gogmagog and Corineus – and they were also at Temple Bar to greet Queen Elizabeth I on the eve of her coronation in 1558.

But Lord Mayor's Day evoked some of the most spectacular pageants of all. The Livery Companies played a major role in the pageants, and for both Lord Mayor's Day and for royal receptions they had special features, often repeated. The speciality of the Goldsmiths' Company was a four-towered castle erected in Cheapside from two sides of which wine poured forth in abundance. The Skinners' Company specialised in a tableau depicting a forest full of wild beasts; and the Grocers' Company portrayed, throughout the seventeenth century, an island of tropical fruits and spices. In 1616, for the Lord Mayor's Day of Sir John Leman (Fishmonger), the Fishmongers' Company excelled themselves with a series of elaborate pageant carriages pulled by chains. These presented eight different tableaux, one being a fishing boat with fishermen who drew up nets full of live fish which they threw to the crowds.

The Lord Mayor's Day river processions between the City and Westminster were inaugurated in the fifteenth century – a magnificent sight, with the barges conveying the Lord Mayor and members of the Livery Companies hung with emblazoned shields, banners and streamers. For 400 years the Lord Mayor's Show remained a combined land and aquatic procession. The gilded Lord Mayor's coach dates from 1757. Prior to 1712 he rode on horseback during the land procession, and then, between 1712 and 1757, he used a less splendid coach than the gilded one in which he rides today.

To return to present-day ceremonies, the Lord Mayor's robes are strictly allocated according to occasion. For Admission Day his robe is of violet silk. For the pageantry of the Lord Mayor's Show he wears a fur-trimmed scarlet robe; and this is the first time that he assumes his Cap of Dignity and the sixteenth-century Chain of Office known as the Lord Mayor's Collar of 'SS'. (Later, as an Alderman who has held office as Lord Mayor, he will wear the Cap of Dignity attached to the right shoulder of his scarlet gown). His Reception Robe is of crimson velvet with miniver fur lining and trimming; it is worn when receiving the Sovereign or Heads of State on a visit to the City. Most splendid of all is the crimson velvet Coronation Robe, trimmed with miniver fur and bands of gold on each front, while the train is edged with gold lace. For the Lord Mayor's Banquet he wears his black and gold robe. On ordinary state occasions the Lord Mayor wears a black silk robe and regalia. He has, despite this variety of robes, only one ceremonial hat – a tricorne with black ostrich plume trimming.

The Badge of Office, the Lord Mayor's Jewel, is a sardonyx cameo portraying the Arms of the City of London encircled by the City's motto, *Domine Dirige Nos*; this, in turn, is encircled by a jewelled wreath of roses, thistles and shamrocks. The Chain of Office is composed of 'S' links interspersed with knots and the Henry VII rose – the flower which combines the roses of both Lancaster and York and symbolises union of the two royal houses through the marriage of Henry VII with Elizabeth of York, daughter of Edward IV. This Collar of 'SS' (pronounced 'esses') is a famous and historic part of the regalia. The right to wear the 'S' ornament is limited to the Lord Mayor of London, the Lord Chief Justice, and to officers of the College of Arms. Before 1594, however, it was also worn by the Lord High Steward, the Lord Chancellor and other royal officers. Various theories have been produced on the signifi-cance of the 'SS' in the Collar, one being that the letters mean 'Seneschallus' (Steward). The office of Lord High Steward of England was held by John of Gaunt, Duke of Lancaster, direct ancestor of Henry Tudor, who ascended the throne as Henry VII. The Collar of 'SS' is known to have been established by John of Gaunt in the fourteenth century. Another suggestion is that the letters derived from the motto *'Souvente me Souvene'* ('Often remember me') borne by the Lady Margaret Beaufort, mother of Henry VII. Yet another – that the letters could stand for *'Sanctus Spiritus'*. The Jewel is suspended from the Collar by a portcullis, the emblem of Henry VII.

It is as important that the Lord Mayor should use the right sword for the appropriate occasion as that he should wear the correct robe. Finest of all is the Pearl Sword, believed to have been the gift of Queen Elizabeth I at the opening of the first Royal Exchange on 23 January 1571; its chased golden handle has as its device Justice and Mercy, and its scabbard is set with pearls. This is the sword which the Lord Mayor presents to the Queen at Temple Bar on her entry to the City of London. There is the City Sword which is carried by the Swordbearer before the Lord Mayor on occasions such as the Court of Common Council in Guildhall; the Mourning Sword or Black Sword is used on occasions of royal mourning; and the Sword of Justice, or Old Bailey Sword, is fixed above the Lord Mayor's seat at the Central Criminal Court, as is the Justice Room Sword in the Mansion House.

The right to have a sword borne before the Mayor was an early privilege granted by the Sovereign and was accompanied by the gift of a royal sword. It is believed that London received its original sword from Edward III, but the first recorded mention of the City Sword was in 1387, and the right to carry it before the Mayor only applied, as today, in the absence of the Sovereign. This is the origin of the custom whereby the sword is surrendered on the approach of the Sovereign to the City – a ceremony first recorded when Richard II was received at the boundary in 1392. When Charles I visited the City in 1641 this ceremony first became a temporary surrender, the sword being returned immediately to the Lord Mayor. Today it is Queen Elizabeth I's Pearl Sword that is surrendered, and the Queen merely touches the hilt.

The Crystal Mace, or City Sceptre – a treasure of great antiquity – is used by the Lord Mayor at the coronation of the Sovereign and at the installation of the new Lord Mayor, when it is handed to him by his predecessor. The Mace carried in civic processions by the Common Cryer and Serjeant-at-Arms is the Great Mace of 1735.

Second only to the Lord Mayor are the two Sheriffs. Like the Lord Mayor, they hold office for one year, and the Guildhall ceremonies of Election and Admission follow very similar lines to those of the Lord Mayor. Their office is the oldest of all, for the Shire-reeve, or Sheriff, existed as early as the seventh century; the office of Portreeve, named in the Charter of William the Conqueror, was the equivalent of Sheriff. Before the creation of the office of Mayor this was the highest office in the City. The right of the citizens to elect their Sheriffs dates from the twelfth century and the task of election has fallen upon the Liverymen of the City since 1475.

On Midsummer Day, 24 June, the Election of Sheriffs takes place. Just as for the Election of the Lord Mayor, up go the Wickets and into formation goes the protective line of Beadles. The procession to the Hustings follows the same pattern as the Mayoral procession, posies are carried and herbs are strewn, while the bed of rose petals in the Livery Hall awaits the City Sword.

Following election, the two Sheriffs receive, in due course, confirmation from the Lord Chancellor on behalf of the Crown, and then, on 28 September, comes Admission Day (the day prior to the Election of the Lord Mayor). For this Shrieval ceremony the reigning Lord Mayor leaves the Mansion House for Guildhall in state, and the whole procedure follows very much the same lines as his own Admission Day, although less prolonged and less impressive. Among the many duties of the Sheriffs is attendance at the Sessions of the Central Criminal Court, and when the Lord Mayor is present on the first two days of each Session the two Sheriffs receive him on the steps of the Old Bailey. One (or both) of the Sheriffs accompanies the Lord Mayor on all ceremonial occasions, and the Sheriffs are responsible for presentation of petitions from the City at the Bar of the House of Commons, for which duty they are attended by the City Remembrancer.

The office of Remembrancer came into being during the reign of Queen Elizabeth I, and it is through him that the City Corporation communicates with the Court and the Ministers of the Crown. He is responsible for the ceremonial of Lord Mayor's Day and for the functions at Guildhall and the Mansion House. On his shoulders, too, falls surveillance that the long-cherished rights and privileges of the City of London are not infringed.

The Livery Companies of the City

In England, as in other countries of Western Europe, the ancient Guilds once held the strings of trade in their hands, and the Livery Companies into which the City of London Guilds evolved served the major purpose of protecting employer and customer through strict training and control of the standard of apprentices; they also had a monopolistic purpose, aimed at cutting out competition from outsiders. Their Courts, in earlier times, handled jurisdiction over members, settled trade disputes, condemned recalcitrant apprentices to be whipped, and fined masters who sinned in ignoring the existing regulations. They also enjoyed a form of self-government that was subject only to the overlordship of the Lord Mayor – just as the Lord Mayor, in his turn, has always ranked second only to the Sovereign in his own territory of the Square Mile.

The Livery Companies no longer exercise overall trade control, but the Goldsmiths, Gunmakers, Apothecaries, Fishmongers and Spectacle Makers still control standards in their particular sphere of trade or craft. The Liverymen serve a vital function in the government of the City and in the election of the Lord Mayor, Sheriffs and Chamberlain, and the Companies' lavish contributions towards education and charity are bestowed with such lack of ostentation that the public in general know little about them.

Membership is composed of Liverymen and Freemen, the right to wear the Livery being restricted to the former, and presiding over each Company, on a basis of annual election, is the Master, together with three or four Wardens. The titles and number of officers varies. For instance, the Goldsmiths, Fishmongers, Dyers and Blacksmiths have a Prime Warden instead of a Master; the Weavers are presided over by an Upper Bailiff. The Clerk is the chief executive officer, and the Beadle, who bears the mace, is prominent in every procession and function of his Livery Company.

The early Guilds were fraternities, and before they possessed their own Halls they met in a church or monastic house in the neighbourhood of their trade or craft. Each adopted as its Patron Saint either the Saint to whom this church was dedicated or the Saint traditionally associated with the particular trade of the Guild or Company. Thus St Dunstan, Patron Saint of metalworkers, became the Patron Saint of the Goldsmiths, and St Peter the Patron Saint of the Fishmongers. For members of these medieval Guilds fear of decease and the wellbeing of their souls was much eased by the assurance of masses and of candles burned on their behalf by fellow members; and at burial they were entitled to use of the Guild's funeral pall. The surviving funeral palls of the Fishmongers, Merchant Taylors, Saddlers and the Parish Clerks are treasured relics and superb examples of the embroiderers' art.

The fraternal origin of the older Companies is reflected in their full titles, still retained though rarely used. The Drapers, for instance, are 'The Master and Wardens and Brethren and Sisters of the Guild or Fraternity of the Blessed Virgin Mary of the Mystery of

Drapers of the City of London'. The word 'Mystery', so often encountered in connection with the early Guilds and Livery Companies,
is said to derive from *métier*, meaning craft or trade. Each year the
members of the Companies met on their Saint's Day in order to
elect their officers and to walk in procession, wearing their Livery,
to attend Divine Service in their church. This is a practice continued
today by most of the Companies.

The palatial Livery Companies' Halls and the grandeur of their
feasts developed with growth in importance and power, and as their
wealth increased so multiplied the many good works which they
undertook – foundation of schools, scholarships, the building of
almshouses, and other charitable works which still form a large
portion of their activities today. Few of the original Halls survived
unscathed the Great Fire of 1666 and the bombs of the last war, but
many of those destroyed or damaged have been rebuilt or restored.
The Master Mariners (whose members must hold a Master Mariner's
certificate) are unique in being the only Livery Company with a
river-borne Hall – the ex-Naval sloop *Wellington*, berthed beside
the Temple Stairs section of the Victoria Embankment.

There are over 80 Livery Companies today, together with two
important and long-established City Companies which do not have
a livery – the Parish Clerks, and the Watermen and Lightermen. The
Saddlers' Company is the oldest, with proof of Anglo-Saxon origin,
and the Weavers claim the earliest Charter, granted by Henry 11
and bearing the signature of St Thomas Becket.

Order of precedence of the Companies was established in the
fifteenth century, and the first 12, strictly graded in order of precedence, are known as the Twelve Great Companies: (1) The Mercers;
(2) The Grocers; (3) The Drapers; (4) The Fishmongers; (5) The
Goldsmiths; (6 and 7) The Merchant Taylors and The Skinners,
two Companies who exchange precedence in alternate years; (8)
The Haberdashers; (9) The Salters; (10) The Ironmongers; (11)
The Vintners; and (12) The Clothworkers.

The City Livery Companies are today on the best of terms, but
in earlier times any sense of fraternity evaporated if activities clashed
or overlapped, and the question of precedence was a real hornet in
the nest. The Skinners were particularly fractious, or so their record

1   The Lord Mayor's Gold Coach conveys the new Lord Mayor through the City streets on Lord Mayor's Day. It is drawn by six powerful Whitbread Shires, and on either side is an escort of Pikemen and Musketeers of the Honourable Artillery Company.

implies. In 1340 conflict between the Skinners and the Fishmongers regarding precedence led to serious bloodshed; then followed strife between the Skinners and the Goldsmiths, and finally between the Skinners and Merchant Taylors. In 1484, following this last feud, the question of precedence was placed before the Lord Mayor for arbitration, and it was decreed that the Merchant Taylors and Skinners should take precedence in alternate years (unless the Lord Mayor Elect should be of either Company) and that each should dine at the other's Hall every year. Peace was restored, and the Skinners and Merchant Taylors have ranked alternately sixth and seventh on terms of friendship ever since.

Among the Livery Companies actively engaged in their original role the predominant example is the Goldsmiths, who still assay gold and silver plate in the Assay Office at Goldsmiths' Hall (origin of the word 'Hallmark'). They also hold the annual Trial of the Pyx, when the coinage of the realm is assayed (see pp. 42–7). The Gunmakers are still active in controlling standards of smallarms, which must be tested in their Proof House. The Fishmongers, under a Charter of James I, still inspect all London's fish at Billingsgate Market, their Inspector and two 'Fishmeters' patrolling to ascertain 'wither the same be wholesome for Man's Body, and fit to be sold or no'. If 'no', they have power to seize it and prevent sale. The Saddlers have powers of search, which means that each year, at quarterly intervals, two Wardens and two members of the Court inspect saddlers' premises within a radius of two miles of London to ensure that their wares are 'well and truly wrought'. The Society of Apothecaries (who founded the Chelsea Physic Garden in 1673) examine and grant the LMSSA Diploma in Medicine, Surgery, Midwifery and Pathology, and also Post Graduate Diplomas in Industrial Health, Medical Jurisprudence, Venereology and History and Philosophy of Medicine and Pharmacy. The Spectacle Makers examine and grant their Fellowship in Ophthalmic Optics and Diploma in Optical Dispensing.

For the coronation of the Queen in 1953 a number of Livery Companies offered special gifts. The Girdlers provided the Girdle of cloth of gold and the Coronation Stole assumed by the Queen during the ceremony; the Gardeners supplied the Coronation bou-

2 (*above*) *Ash Wednesday Cakes and Ale custom, Stationers' Hall.*
3 (*below*) *Trial of the Pyx – members of the Jury count the coins.*

quet; the Glovers provided the Coronation glove which the Queen wore on her right hand during the ceremony – in continuation of an ancient manorial custom by Grand Serjeanty previously exercised by the Lord of the Manor of Worksop; the Tallow Chandlers provided the candles.

The Lord Mayor of London receives certain traditional presentations from the Livery Companies. Each January the Master of the Butchers' Company makes a personal presentation of a Boar's Head, a custom which dates from 1342. In that year the City granted land adjoining the River Fleet to the butchers of the Parish of St Nicholas (where the Shambles, or butchers' quarter, was situated) on condition that they maintain a wharf and present a Boar's Head to the Lord Mayor every year. This grant was especially beneficial in the eyes of the medieval butchers, for it enabled them to clean their meat in the river. The Gardeners' Company make an annual presentation of vegetables to the Lord Mayor; and each November the Fruiterers' Company present fruits – a custom which originated in medieval times. In those early days the 'Fruit Meters' (an office purchased from the Lord Mayor) were granted the right to claim tolls in money or produce from the cartloads of fruit entering the City of London. This caused friction, and the unrest came to a head when, in 1748, 'cherries from beyond the sea' came to the gate of the City to be sold. The Freemen of the Fruiterers not only resented the toll itself but demanded that, if pay they must, *their* payment should be less than that of 'the stranger'. The dispute resulted in abolition of the hated Meter men, and the custom was established of an annual presentation to the Lord Mayor himself. This is today composed of fruits from all parts of the United Kingdom and other parts of the world – a superb display which is later distributed to hospitals and old age pensioners. On the same day the Lord Mayor entertains the Court of the Fruiterers' Company to a State Dinner in the Mansion House, and as the Loving Cup passes around it is clear that the Meter men and the friction they aroused are no more than a distant memory.

Ceremonial which has survived through the ages among the Livery Companies is the passing of the Loving Cup at their Dinners. The ritual is believed to stem from the assassination (in AD 978) of

King Edward the Martyr at the royal hunting lodge which was the predecessor of Corfe Castle in Dorset. This dastardly murder was planned by the King's stepmother, Elfrida, with the object of placing her own son, Ethelred (later known as the Unready) upon the throne. The deed was done while Elfrida offered a stirrup cup to the King and his hands were not free for defence. It became customary thereafter to adopt a protective measure when passing a cup of wine along the table at gatherings, and while a man drank, holding the cup with both hands, his neighbour stood with drawn sword beside him. As practised today the Loving Cup ritual differs little, except for the absence of the sword. Three members rise simultaneously – one who drinks, one who holds the Loving Cup cover, and a third who usually stands back to back with the drinker and is the traditional defender. On receiving the Loving Cup, the man about to drink turns to his neighbour and they bow to each other. The latter removes the cover, and after the former has drunk the rim is wiped with a napkin, the cover replaced, they bow once more, and only when his role in the ceremony is completed does the first of the trio resume his seat.

Especially notable are the Cockayne silver gilt Loving Cups of the Skinners' Company, five in number, all in the shape of cocks with removable heads and obviously a play on the donor's name, for they were bequeathed by Mr William Cockayne in 1598 – 'fyve Cuppes to the said Master, Wardens and Company of Skynners and their successors forever, to choose the Masters and Wardens with'. The Barbers' Company possess a remarkable Loving Cup, presented by King Charles II in 1676, which celebrates the Boscobel Oak in whose branches the King sought refuge from the Cromwellian soldiers; its stem depicts the trunk of an oak, while leaves, branches and silver acorns ornament the cup, and the cover is a crown. The Clothworkers have a much prized Loving Cup which was the gift of Samuel Pepys, Master in 1677. The Drapers have a Loving Cup presented in 1578 by William Lambarde, the antiquary, historian and author of *The Perambulation of Kent* and other works. The Broderers have two cups presented by royal embroiderers – one of 1606 from John Parr, embroiderer to Elizabeth I and James I the other of 1628 from Edmund Harrison, embroiderer to James I and Charles I. The Mercers (first in precedence of the Great Twelve and the Livery Company of the famous Richard Whittington) have the splendid Leigh Cup presented in 1554 and inscribed: 'To elect the Master of the Mercerie hither am I sent, and by Sir Thomas Leigh for the same intent.' The Goldsmiths, although their collection of plate is magnificent and includes the cup used by Queen Elizabeth I at her Coronation Banquet, do not practise the Loving Cup ceremonial, neither do they walk in procession on election day.

The ritual originally followed at the election feasts involved the crowning of the new Master and Wardens with 'garlands' or crowns, a custom still practised by some of the Companies. A record of the Drapers' Company of 1546 states that in the middle of the election feast the first Warden, coming out of the parlour with the minstrels, approached the high table where the retiring Master was seated and passed to him the garland. He forthwith tried it on the head of others at the table, finally discovering the right fit on the head of the new Master.

Although the charade of trying the Master's garland or crown on various heads no longer takes place, the crowning ceremonies practised by the Companies today are based on this early ritual, and as an example I will describe the election day ceremony of the Girdlers. The procession enters with musicians playing Handel's March from *Scipio* on oboe and flute, and the Beadle leads the bearer of the crowns followed by the Clerk and the Butler with the Loving Cup. The procession halts before the new Master, the Clerk announces his name and, taking the crown from the cushion on which it rests, places it on his head. The newly crowned Master then drinks from the Loving Cup, pledges the Livery, and gives thanks for his election. The ceremony is repeated for each Warden, and finally the procession, after circulating the hall, retires. Until the last war the Girdlers retained their early crowns – the richly embroidered Master's crown dating from 1575. In 1941 they were destroyed by enemy action, and although replicas have been made they are a sad loss.

Among other Livery Companies who retain the crowning ceremony are the Carpenters, Drapers, Fishmongers, Haberdashers, Leathersellers, Parish Clerks, Pewterers, and the Skinners. The Barbers no longer wear their garlands at the installation ceremony, but they possess very fine ones and at their dinners these are held by the Master and Wardens during the reception. The Master's garland is of 1670 and consists of a crown-shaped silver-gilt circlet mounted on red velvet, the design incorporating the same theme of oak leaves and acorns as does their Royal Oak Loving Cup.

The Brewers preserve three seventeenth-century Wardens' crowns but do not use them ceremonially, and this also applies to the Broderers' Company, whose seventeenth-century crowns are richly ornamented with silver-gilt and silver thread embroidery. The Carpenters' Company still use a Master's crown of 1561 with Wardens' crowns of the seventeenth century; and the Haberdashers use their Master's garland of *c.* 1530 and Wardens' garlands at their Publication Ceremony (as their election ceremony is called) and in Court. For the election day of the Skinners' Company (on Corpus Christi Day) the Master's and Wardens' caps are used together with the Cockayne series of silver cock Loving Cups – a ritual known as the Cocks and Caps Ceremony. The procession enters the hall led by the Band, with ten Liverymen bearing the five Caps and the five Cocks – the treasured Cockayne Loving Cups which are only used once a year for this crowning ceremony.

The Installation Ceremony of the Parish Clerks is of special interest. The new Master is elected on Ascension Day but is not crowned until the July Installation Court, and the Company is unique in having two Masters' crowns. Until 1639 there were two Masters, serving concurrently, and the two crowns are now worn by the Retiring and Incoming Masters at the ceremony. Until recently the original embroidered crowns of 1601 were still in use, but now, owing to their frailty, replicas have been made. The originals are, at the time of writing, in the care of the Victoria and Albert Museum, but their final home may be the new Museum of London. The funeral pall of the Parish Clerks, another treasured relic, is also at present at the Victoria and Albert Museum. Greatest treasure of all, however, is the Bede Roll, preserved in the archives of the Guildhall Library. This is a prayer or obituary roll which records names of members between 1449 and 1521 who were prepared to offer prayers for the faithful departed – for kings and ecclesiastical dignitaries as well as deceased brethren – and the custom is still retained in the corporate worship of the Parish Clerks and in their Silent Toast: 'To the immortal and pious memory of King Henry vi, King Edward iv, King James i, and King Charles i, also of William Roper and Richard Hust, and all other benefactors of this ancient Guild and all Brethren departed this life. May their souls through the mercy of God rest in peace'.

This City Company is of thirteenth-century origin; as a religious Guild it bore the title of the Fraternity of St Nicholas, and its first Charter was granted by Henry vi in 1442. It is not a Livery Company, always having preferred the distinction of wearing the surplice to a livery. At the Michaelmas Service in St Lawrence Jewry, which takes place prior to election of the new Lord Mayor in Guildhall, the Master of the Parish Clerks, attended by his Wardens, is crucifer. It is the custom of the Parish Clerks to toast one another by the names of their parishes, not by their names. After dinner their musical tradition is kept alive by singing a hymn half in English and half in Latin in praise of the Church and the City.

During the election day Court procedure of the Saddlers' Company an ornate Ballot Box of curious construction continues to serve its centuries' old role. This Ballot Box was made in 1619 for the East India Company and was acquired by the Saddlers with sufficient speed to have been in use for the annual election of the Master and Wardens since 1619. Its special quality is that when the hand is put into the aperture, the wrist can be turned so that the ball drops into the appropriate voting drawer without being discerned by onlookers. Possibly the East India Company scrapped the Ballot Box for this very reason, preferring a show of hands and knowledge which way people were voting.

Two of the most important customs associated with the Livery Companies are Swan Upping (the Vintners and the Dyers) and Doggett's Coat and Badge Race (the Fishmongers, and the Watermen and Lightermen). These are described in the section *Customs of London's River*.

The Stationers' Company have a long-established Ash Wednesday custom in the Cakes and Ale distribution which takes place in Stationers' Hall on that day. This stems from a bequest of 1612 by a member, John Norton – a benefactor who bequeathed funds to cover purchase of a property in Wood Street and the preaching of a sermon each Ash Wednesday in the Chapel of St Faith, in the Crypt of St Paul's Cathedral (now the Chapel of the Order of the British Empire); in addition he provided a sum to cover cakes and ale in perpetuity as refreshment before or after the service. So on the morning of Ash Wednesday members assemble in Stationers' Hall to partake of John Norton's ale and freshly baked cakes. The latter used to be large brown spiced cakes which were cut into slices, but they now take the form of deliciously hot spiced buns. In the afternoon a procession forms, with the Court robed, and sets out for the Cathedral and John Norton's sermon.

Another Stationers' member and benefactor, Richard Johnson, is remembered each year by the 'Bubble Sermon'. He died in the eighteenth century, leaving money for the poor of the Company and to provide for an annual sermon, the subject to be, without variation, *Bulla est vita humana*. Each year, therefore, on the first Tuesday in June, the members of the Company gather to honour their benefactor and to listen to the sermon, its theme translated as 'Life is a bubble'. The service is held in the Church of St Martin-within-Ludgate, to which members walk in procession. This church stands on the south side of the Garden Court of Stationers' Hall and is adjacent to the site of the old gate, Ludgate, western boundary of the former walled city. So close 'within the wall' were the church and the Hall that a room in Stationers' Hall, now known as the Card Room, was built into one of the bastions – for which, until the 1950s, the Company paid a peppercorn rent to the City Corporation.

The Stationers, who restrict membership very rigidly to the trade, still bind apprentices. In former times they had the sole right to print Almanacks, a monopoly held for centuries, and the earliest preserved in Stationers' Hall is of 1620. The Company also controlled registration of copyright until this ceased to be compulsory under the 1911 Act, and the early copyright registrations held at Stationers' Hall are of the greatest interest today; they include over 20 of Shakespeare's works, together with Milton's *Paradise Lost* and Dr Johnson's *Dictionary*. In their Garden Court is a tall plane tree, and there is a peculiarity about this tree that is worth relating. Its roots thrive in the ashes of heretical books which, in past days, were condemned by the ecclesiastical authorities and were burned in this courtyard by the Master and Wardens of the Stationers' Company.

The Clothworkers' Company have a custom at their Dinners which could be mystifying to guests unless forewarned. During the Dinner the waiters ask, 'Do you dine, Sir, with Alderman or Lady Cooper?' If the decision is to dine with Alderman Cooper, brandy will be provided; to accept the hospitality of Lady Cooper results in Hollands Gin. Alderman and Lady Cooper lived in the seventeenth century, and the origin of this custom is said to have been the sudden collapse and death of Alderman Cooper after dining at Clothworkers' Hall. The potency of the excellent brandy was blamed, and Lady Cooper provided funds to ensure that, in perpetuity, Hollands Gin be offered as an alternative at their dinners.

The Vintners' Company still fulfil a ruling laid down many centuries ago that, on Installation Day, the Company's tackle porters (wine porters) shall sweep the road 'with full besoms' between Vintners' Hall and their Church 'in order that the Master, Wardens, and Brethren of the Court of Assistants step not in any foulness or litter in our streets and further that each Master, Warden or Brother of the Court of Assistants be provided with a nosegay of sweet and fine herbs that their nostrils be not offended by any noxious flavours or other ill-vapours'. To this day, therefore, the procession leaves Vintners' Hall on Installation Day and proceeds to the Church of St James Garlickhythe – the Master, Wardens and Court of Assistants carrying their nosegays while a tackle porter sweeps the road ahead. There used to be more than one tackle porter for the sweeping operation, always dressed traditionally in white smocks and black silk top hats. Today the occupation of tackle porter no longer exists, and only one of the original porters survives; clad in his white smock and 'topper' he carries out the task alone.

Trial of the Pyx

Goldsmiths' Hall, Foster Lane
Trial, February or March; Verdict, May

The Trial of the Pyx, and the subsequent Pyx Luncheon at which the

Verdict is announced, represent an ancient custom of great importance to the nation. By means of this Trial an independent check is made on the accuracy of composition and weight of the coins of the realm. The word 'Pyx' means Mint Box.

Some form of coin testing was undertaken in Saxon times and possibly as early as the Roman Occupation, but it was during Henry II's reign (1154–1189) that regular tests of the coinage were introduced, together with reorganization of the various Mints which existed throughout the country. The first reference to a trial plate (the standard to which the coinage must conform) occurs in the reforms of Henry II.

By the thirteenth century the Trial of the Pyx had already begun to take the form that we know today, as shown in Henry III's writ of 1248 to the Mayor and citizens of London, entrusting them 'to elect twelve of the more discreet and lawful men of our city of London and join with them twelve good goldsmiths of the same city, making twenty-four discreet men in all, who shall go before the Barons of our Exchequer at Westminster and examine, upon oath, together with the Barons, both the old and the new money of our land, and make provision how it may be bettered; and that it be made of good silver, and that it be lawful and for the good of the realm'.

The earliest surviving trial plate is of silver and dates from 1279 (reign of Edward I). It is preserved at the Royal Mint, and is unique in being the only trial plate shaped in the form of an ingot. In this same year of 1279 William de Turnemire was appointed 'Master-Moneyer' or Master of the Mint, in order that uniform control be provided over the Mints, both Royal and Episcopal, dispersed throughout the kingdom. The Ordinance which brought this about stated: 'First a standard must be made which will remain at the Exchequer or in such place as our lord the king will. And the money shall be made according to the form of the standard and of the same fineness as the standard'. Sample coins were to be placed in Pyx chests, and these were to be independently checked. In other words, the procedure of the Trial of the Pyx, as carried out today, had come into being.

Early Trials of the Pyx were held, first in Westminster Hall, then in the Star Chamber, and later in the Exchequer at Westminster. It was not until 1870, as laid down in the Coinage Act of that year, that Goldsmiths' Hall became the established venue of the Trial, although certain special Trials of the Pyx had already been held there. The 1870 Act also decreed that the annual Trial be presided over by the Queen's Remembrancer; prior to this it was the Lord Chancellor's responsibility to authorise the Trials and to preside over them.

An interesting relic which has survived from earlier Trials of the Pyx is a chart, dated 1496, which used to hang in the Star Chamber. From this it is seen that at the end of the fifteenth century the ear of wheat still provided the standard unit for weighing the coins. In the sixteenth century not only was the standard of weights improved but Queen Elizabeth I directed, by Warrant under the Great Seal, that responsibility for the Trial of the Pyx should rest with 'My friends The Wardens of the mystery of Goldsmiths of the City of London'.

As already mentioned, there were from time to time special Trials of the Pyx. One of these was held in 1537 on Archbishop Cranmer's request that the coins from the Episcopal Mint in Canterbury be assayed. The Trial was ordered by Thomas Cromwell, then Chancellor of the Exchequer, and was held in Goldsmiths' Hall instead of at Westminster.

The Trial of the Pyx has only rarely been attended by the Sovereign in person, but in 1611 King James I was present at the Trial with his eldest son, Prince Henry; King Charles I, following his father's example, also came to observe the Trial in operation.

For many centuries the Pyx Chamber at Westminster Abbey was the storage place of the all-important trial plates. This continued until 1843, when the office of the Queen's Assay Master in the Royal Mint became the depository. Today, when the Trial takes place, gold, silver and cupro-nickel trial plates are produced by the Standards Department of the Board of Trade, and in addition the Royal Mint, the Treasury and the Goldsmiths' Company each have their own portions. From these plates it is established that the coins of the realm conform to the exact standard of size, weight and metallic content.

In the past the trial plates have caused occasional crises, one occurring in 1657 when two missing plates caused the Trial to be postponed. It 1681 all previous trial plates possessed by the Goldsmiths' Company were destroyed in a fire which burnt the Assay

Office to the ground, and the earliest now held by the Goldsmiths' Company are, therefore, those of 1688. Another dilemma was when the Verdict proved unsatisfactory – but the trial plate proved to be in error and not the coin. And during another Trial over-enthusiastic building up of the furnace caused the whole furnace chimney to catch fire. On the whole, however, it is rare for the Trial and the subsequent Verdict to run other than smoothly.

In 1966 Britain finally decided to change to decimal currency at the rate of 100 new pence to the pound, and Decimal Day was fixed for 15 February 1971. On this day six new decimal coins came into use – the bronze ½p, 1p, 2p, and the cupro-nickel 5p, 10p and 50p; the old sixpence was temporarily retained at the value of 2½p.

It was this change to decimal coinage, and the vast minting operation involved, that made the Tower Hill premises of the Royal Mint inadequate and resulted in the establishment of the massive new Royal Mint at Llantrisant in South Wales. The London Mint (originally at Westminster) had been established within the Tower of London in 1300, and it had continued to produce the coins of the realm within the fortress walls until, in 1811, the imposing Royal Mint building on Tower Hill was completed. Now tradition has been broken, and this great new Mint, so far from the capital, has become for most of us merely a money-making factory instead of part of London's history. The Mint building beside the Tower is, however, being preserved as a museum of coinage.

The decimalization which brought this change about was seriously contemplated many times in the past, and Sir Isaac Newton, appointed Master of the Mint in 1699, was a strong advocate; but a new coinage had been introduced three years earlier, in 1696, and it was inconceivable that another change should be made so soon. Had Sir Isaac been Master of the Mint in 1696 it is believed that he would never have condoned the new coinage in its non-decimal form. It was in 1848 that the first definite step towards decimalization was taken – with the introduction of the florin. This was intended to replace the half-crown, but the half-crown gained a reprieve and continued to exist alongside the florin until the 1971 decimalization. The first florin of 1848 was known as the 'Godless' florin owing to omission of the words *Dei Gratia* – an omission which Queen Victoria speedily rectified. Sets of decimal coins were actually made in 1857, 1859 and 1918 – so decimalization, when it eventually came, was something that had been pending for a long time.

There has been little change in the procedure of the Trial of the Pyx as the centuries have passed. It is still, as decreed by King Henry III in 1248, handled by a chosen Jury of discreet men, Freemen of the Goldsmiths' Company and many of them leaders of the financial world of the City of London.

The first portion of the Trial, the counting, usually occupies the morning, but on the occasion which followed decimalization so many decimal coins had been minted during the period prior to the Trial that the counting – which should have finished at lunchtime – continued into the afternoon. At the start of the Trial the coins for assay are held in Pyx boxes lined up against the wall of the Court Room in Goldsmiths' Hall. These coins have been put aside throughout the past year by the Mint Foremen, who are responsible for taking one coin from every batch minted. The Pyx boxes contain the coins in sealed bags, each bag holding 50.

At the commencement of the Trial the Jury sit round the table and members of the Mint staff stand beside the Pyx boxes. Before each member of the Jury are placed two bowls, one of copper and the other of wood. Then the Queen's Remembrancer enters, an imposing figure in wig and gown, and on the announcement 'Pray silence for the Queen's Remembrancer' he makes his opening speech. The names of the Jury are then called over, they take the oath, a Foreman is appointed, and the Trial begins.

The Pyx boxes are opened and the sealed bags of coins are distributed. Each member of the Jury has been supplied with a pair of scissors in addition to his twin bowls. He cuts off the top of the bag, retains the numbered seal section as a check, and then counting starts. One coin from each bag of 50 coins is taken at random and placed in the copper bowl; the remaining 49 coins, having been counted, are placed in the wooden bowl. The contents of the two bowls are then promptly removed and the next sealed bag embarked upon; it is the single coin in each Jury member's copper bowl that is taken for assay. Downstairs the weighing starts, after which the coins are taken to the Assay Office in Goldsmiths' Hall.

The packaging of the coins in special sealed bags is to avoid coins falling out. Some years ago one coin was missing following the counting, and this caused great consternation. Calm was restored when the missing coin came to light in the trouser turn-up of an elderly member of the Jury.

One concession to modern times has been introduced, for half the total coins brought to the Trial are now tipped into a coin-counting machine and this speeds up proceedings considerably. Nevertheless, the other half is still handled in the traditional way by the Jury, so that we find, to this day, men of great eminence in the financial world taking their places round the Jury table, scissors in hand and bowls before them, carefully snipping bags open and meticulously counting the coins by hand.

An interval of some eight weeks or so elapses while the assay is carried out. Then, in May, the Trial is reconvened, and the Queen's Remembrancer returns to Goldsmiths' Hall to ask the Jury for their Verdict. If no complication has arisen proceedings are short, and once the Verdict has been given the Jury and guests retire to the Livery Hall for the Pyx Luncheon, at which the Chancellor of the Exchequer, as Master of the Mint, is always the principal speaker.

The Pyx Luncheon brings the Trial of the Pyx to a close. The 'discreet men' disperse, returning to their posts of dignity throughout the City where, most certainly, they will not be required to wield the scissors and count the coins in person until another year has passed. And at the Royal Mint the Foremen will already have set about refilling the Pyx boxes with a single coin from each batch minted.

Ceremony of the Knollys Rose

The Mansion House (on or near 24 June)

The presentation of a red rose to the Lord Mayor of London on St John the Baptist's Day (24 June) is a ceremony dating back 600 years. It proves that town planners existed as early as the fourteenth century, and that then, as now, permission must be gained to build within the confines of the City of London.

In 1370, while the French wars of the fourteenth century still raged and as the reign of Edward III was drawing to a close, two forces were sent from England to France. One was under the leadership of John of Gaunt, Duke of Lancaster, and the other was led by Sir Robert Knollys. His wife, the Lady Constance Knollys, was left in their home in Seething Lane in the Parish of All Hallows Berkyngecherche near the Tower. It happened that there was a threshing ground on the opposite side of the Lane, and the chaff blew towards the Knollys property when the wind was so inclined. This was far from agreeable to the Lady Constance – and she was a woman of action. Despite Sir Robert's absence she purchased the property opposite, transformed the land into a rose garden, and in order to avoid descending to the muddy soil of Seething Lane she built a foot bridge (or *haut-pas* in the language of the time).

Sir Robert Knollys returned from the wars – and was horrified. As a close friend of the Mayor, Sir William Walworth, he was well aware of the building restrictions which prevailed and the outcome was exactly as he feared. He and the Lady Constance were cited in the Mayor's Court on a charge of having built a footbridge contrary to the existing laws and regulations; and there was no alternative to a declaration of guilt and imposition of the appropriate penalty. But what appropriate penalty could Sir William Walworth inflict upon his friend, remembering his valiant record of fighting and leadership in France? The dilemma was nicely solved, the penance being that Sir Robert Knollys and the Lady Constance, their heirs and assigns, render for ever one red rose on the Feast of St John the Baptist.

The house in Seething Lane and the offending footbridge exist no more, but there is still a rose garden in the Lane; and from this garden a red rose is plucked and presented to the Lord Mayor in the Mansion House on the appropriate day each year. If the garden fails to produce a perfect bloom, then one is obtained elsewhere, but usually the red rose does come from Seething Lane.

There has only been one break (amounting to several decades) in the rendering of the Knollys Rose; otherwise the ceremony has continued faithfully since 1381. It was the Reverend P. B. Clayton (better known as Tubby Clayton, Founder Padre of Toc H and Vicar of the Church of All Hallows-by-the-Tower) who revived the custom; and to ensure its continuation after his death he entrusted responsibility to the Court of the Company of Watermen and Lightermen. For this reason the Watermen lend colour to the presentation, and the Bargemaster, with eight winners of Doggett's Coat and Badge Race, form a guard of honour on either side of the Saloon of the Mansion House. The Lord Mayor and Lady Mayoress stand before the dual thrones as the procession approaches, led by the Verger of the Church of All Hallows-by-the-Tower, who bears, on a blue altar cushion, a superb and unblemished red rose. Accompanying him is the Chief Escort to the Rose (always some-one of eminence in the City to whom the invitation is extended), and he, after a short speech, presents the rose to the Lord Mayor. The procession includes the Master and Clerk of the Company of Water-men and Lightermen and the Vicar of All Hallows-by-the-Tower. And thus the penalty of 1381, earned by the headstrong Lady Con-stance Knollys, is rendered 'for ever'.

Lloyd's of London – the Lutine Bell and other customs

Lime Street, E.C.3

There are two misconceptions about Lloyd's of London: (1) that it is an insurance company, and (2) that the Lutine Bell is rung when a ship sinks. But Lloyd's is far removed from being an insurance company – it is an international insurance market and the world centre of marine intelligence; and although the Lutine Bell was originally rung on the sinking of a large vessel, it is now *never* rung when a ship sinks. One stroke of the bell denotes that a ship is over-due or missing, and two strokes means safe arrival. If a ship sinks or is badly damaged, the details are entered in the Loss Book – but the bell does not toll. Navigational aids and marine intelligence are so efficient nowadays that the Lutine Bell is only rung occasionally each year, but when its stroke is heard it brings instant silence to the hubbub of Lloyd's – for the one stroke still means misfortune and two strokes good news. The bell also tolls its two strokes on ceremonial occasions – such as, for instance, the visit of the Prince of Wales to Lloyd's in November 1970.

La Lutine was a French ship launched in 1785 and captured by the British at Toulon in 1793. Renamed *Lutine* she joined the British Fleet, and was carrying a cargo of money and bullion (insured at Lloyd's) when, on the night of 10 October 1799, she was wrecked off the coast of Holland, between the islands of Vlieland and Terschelling. All lives were lost, and the cargo went down with the ship. The Lutine Bell (weight 106 lbs and diameter $17\frac{1}{2}$ inches) was salvaged in 1859.

The Lloyd's Loss Book is as traditional as the Lutine Bell, and each entry is still made meticulously with a quill pen – a custom which does not, however, mean an obsession with the past; Lloyd's was, in fact, the first City institution to use computers.

Another tradition is the Underwriters' desks, known as 'boxes', each consisting of a high-backed bench and table similar to the seating in Edward Lloyd's coffee house in Tower Street – the humble starting point of this mighty organisation. In the seventeenth century the coffee houses of London were popular gathering places for debate and for commercial transactions. So it came about that Edward Lloyd's coffee house, owing to its proximity to London's river, was much patronised by men with seafaring connections, including shipowners who met there the individual merchant underwriters who were the predecessors of the Lloyd's syndicates of today. Edward Lloyd's coffee house thus gained a reputation for being the best place in which to arrange marine insurance cover, and Edward Lloyd saw to it that the latest shipping information was available, brought to his coffee house by runners from the waterfront. His news sheet, known as *Lloyd's News*, was first printed in 1696 and can therefore be regarded as the distant ancestor of Lloyd's daily newspaper, *Lloyd's List*.

At Lloyd's today the liveried doormen, known as 'Waiters', wear a red coat (referred to as a cloak) with a wide black collar, together with a black silk top hat ornamented with gold braid and white gloves. The other liveried staff, also Waiters, wear a navy blue tail coat with a red collar and silver buttons; the Head Waiter is distinguished by a blue instead of a red collar. The man who sits beneath the Lutine

4   (above) *Beating the Bounds at the Tower of London.*
5   (below) *Distribution of the Maundy Money. The Queen leaves Westminster Abbey after the Royal Maundy Service.*

Bell is known as the Caller, and he wears the same red-coated (or red-cloaked) livery as the doormen. It is the Caller who rings the Lutine Bell, but his main occupation is calling out the names of brokers as required. The role of the Caller dates back to the days of the coffee house, when a boy known as 'the Kidney' called out the notices.

A treasured heritage at Lloyd's is the Nelson Room (on the gallery floor of the Underwriting Room) where many Nelson relics are displayed together with swords and other awards made by Lloyd's Patriotic Fund. Here, too, is the log book of HMS *Euryalus*, written from hour to hour during the Battle of Trafalgar and containing Nelson's famous signalled message: 'England expects that every man will do his duty.'

6   *Coronation of Queen Elizabeth II – the moment of crowning.*

CHAPTER TWO

The Monarchy

Coronation

For antiquity of ceremonial and sheer splendour of pageantry nothing compares with the coronation of the Sovereign. Every coronation has taken place at Westminster since 1066 saw the crowning of Harold II and William I – the last Saxon and first Norman Kings. But the Abbey is not, of course, the same building today. In the thirteenth century Henry III rebuilt the Minster almost entirely, his ambition being to provide a shrine worthy of the bones of Edward the Confessor and an Abbey glorious enough to merit that shrine. He died before its completion, and the present Abbey continued to evolve up to the eighteenth century.

The usual interval between accession to the throne and coronation is, today, one year. In earlier times, however, when accession had been won by battle or was open to dispute, the new Sovereign wasted little time in assuming the crown. The Battle of Hastings was fought on 14 October 1066, and the Conqueror did not allow more than a couple of months to elapse before the crown was safely on his head. Similarly the victor of the Battle of Bosworth in 1485, the first Tudor King, Henry VII, was crowned in the Abbey with the minimum of delay.

Throughout the centuries the coronations at Westminster have not been free of ill omen. Richard I, named Coeur de Lion for his exploits in the Third Crusade, was not a particularly successful monarch at home; he was disloyal to his father, Henry II; his coronation was accompanied by a massacre of the Jews; his imprisonment when captured by Leopold, Duke of Austria, cost the country large sums drawn from the pockets of the people for his ransom; and he was killed, ingloriously, by an ill-aimed arrow shot by one of his own marksmen. It may, therefore, have been truly an ill omen that a bat swooped around his head in the Abbey as he assumed the crown (1189). Richard II, doomed to abdication and assassination, lost a shoe as he left the Abbey after the crowning in 1377. James II's crown wobbled and nearly fell during the coronation procession to Westminster Hall in 1685 – and his short reign ended in flight.

The most undignified scene at a coronation was created in 1821 by George IV's alienated Queen, Caroline of Brunswick. Barred from the Abbey on the orders of her husband, she made her way to a side entrance where the doorkeeper, true to his instructions, refused entry.

The Coronation Banquet in Westminster Hall used to be one of the great events of the coronation festivities, and when this was discontinued (the last was at George IV's coronation) two famous hereditary customs came to an end. These were the Challenge of the King's Champion, and the carrying of the monarch's canopy by the Barons of the Cinque Ports.

The hereditary duty of the King's Champion involved riding on horseback, in full armour, into the presence of the coronation assembly at the Banquet, then challenging to mortal combat any who might dispute the right and title of the Sovereign. The office of Hereditary Grand Champion of England has been held for many centuries by the Dymokes of Scrivelsby in Lincolnshire, and until the nineteenth century this Challenge provided one of the most dramatic moments of the Coronation Banquet. There have, however, been one or two mishaps during the Challenge. At James II's coronation the Champion, on dismounting to kiss the King's hand in homage, slipped and fell, and with the weight of his armour it was some time before he could be got to his feet again. And at the coronation of George III, although the Champion performed his role most excellently, one of his companions, Lord Talbot, effectively destroyed the dignity of the scene by riding into Westminster Hall backwards; he had trained his horse so assiduously to back out of the Hall after the Challenge that the animal refused any other form of progress.

On the last occasion when the Challenge was undertaken (George iv's coronation) there were no mishaps. The Champion entered the great Hall impressively, his armour gleaming and his horse richly caparisoned, while riding beside him were the Deputy Earl Marshal, Lord Howard of Effingham, and the Lord High Constable, the Duke of Wellington, each wearing ceremonial robes and coronet. Three times the trumpet sounded, and then the voice of Garter King of Arms proclaimed the Challenge – to any person of what degree soever, high or low, the Champion was 'ready in person to combat with him, on what day soever shall be appointed'. The Champion threw down the gauntlet, which was duly restored to him by Garter, and thereupon the procedure was repeated in the middle of the Hall and again at the foot of the steps before the throne. No combatant having come forward, the King drank to the Champion from a gold cup which was then delivered to him. He, in turn, drank from it and then left the Hall, taking with him the cup with its golden cover as his rightful trophy. Today, although this picturesque ceremony of the Challenge has lapsed, the Hereditary Champion is given other coronation duties. Mr Frank S. Dymoke carried the Standard of England at the coronations of Edward vii, George v and George vi. Colonel John Dymoke, the present Hereditary Grand Champion, carried the Union Standard at Queen Elizabeth ii's coronation in 1953.

The Barons of the Cinque Ports long held the honour of carrying the canopy held over the Sovereign's head when he walked in procession at his coronation. Prior to the creation of the Royal Navy this ancient maritime confederation guarded the Channel Coast and Channel crossing, and the Head Ports were Hastings, Romney, Hythe, Dover and Sandwich, with the later addition of Rye and Winchelsea bringing the number of Head Ports up to seven. Matthew Paris, in 1236, described the coronation of Henry iii's Queen Eleanor in the following words: 'The Barons of the Cinque Ports carried over the King wherever he went the silken cloth four-square, purple, supported by four silvered spears with four little silver-gilt bells, four Barons being assigned to every spear . . .' The canopy, the decorative bells and the silver staves were divided between the Cinque Ports after each coronation, and examples are still preserved in the museums of the Cinque Ports. In early times Freemen of the

Ports all bore the title 'Baron of the Cinque Ports', but today it is only held by the Freemen who attend a coronation. Since the last ceremonial carrying of the canopy in 1821 the Barons of the Cinque Ports have been given places of honour and duties at each coronation, but the canopy, staves and bells, which were so valued a trophy, are no more.

Many months before the coronation another important and traditional ceremony takes place. After the death of a Sovereign the Proclamation of the successor to the throne is made within about 48 hours. The Heralds assemble on the Friary Court balcony of St James's Palace clad in their tabards of scarlet, blue and gold quartered with the Royal Arms. These men of medieval aspect are the Kings of Arms – Garter, Clarenceux and Norroy; also Windsor, Richmond, Somerset, Lancaster, York and Chester Heralds; and Pursuivants Rouge Croix, Bluemantle, Rouge Dragon and Portcullis. With them is the Earl Marshal, who holds hereditary responsibility for all State ceremonial. A fanfare by the State Trumpeters draws all eyes to the balcony, and Garter King of Arms pronounces the Proclamation – in 1952, that '. . . the high and mighty Princess Elizabeth Alexandra Mary is now become our Sovereign Liege Lady Elizabeth II, by the Grace of God Queen of Great Britain and Northern Ireland and of all her other Realms and Territories . . .' The words 'God save the Queen' and a further trumpet call ended the ceremony. Then the Heralds retired from the balcony and proceeded to the other London Proclamation sites – Charing Cross, Temple Bar, and the steps of the Royal Exchange in the City, where the ceremony was repeated.

In writing of the actual coronation ceremony I cannot do better than describe the one closest to our memories. On 2 June 1953 Queen Elizabeth II was crowned in Westminster Abbey, and never has there been a happier or more brilliant example of the coronation ceremonial. There was no ill omen on that day – no bat swooped in the Abbey, no shoe was lost in the Procession, no Champion slipped and fell, there was no wobbling of the crown. The only hitch, if it can be called one, was at 7 o'clock in the morning when the horses of a peer's carriage, trotting amiably down Whitehall, stopped unpredictably at Downing Street instead of proceeding to the Abbey.

For five minutes the horses stood their ground, while liveried coach-
men tugged and coaxed; then, equally unpredictably, they set off
at a trot for the Abbey.

From the moment that the Gold Coach emerged from the gates
of Buckingham Palace, the day was one of unparalleled splendour,
solemnity and rejoicing – although one has to own that the weather
did not co-operate. The progress to the Abbey included nine massive
processions – a vast scene of pageantry provided by the Armed
Forces of the Homeland and the Commonwealth. In their traditional
place close to the Sovereign marched the Queen's Bodyguard of the
Yeomen of the Guard, resplendent in their scarlet Tudor uniforms;
and walking ahead of the Gold Coronation Coach was the Queen's
Bargemaster together with 12 Royal Watermen. The Lord Mayor's
Gold Coach was escorted by the armour-clad Pikemen and Musketeers of the Honourable Artillery Company.

The coronation ceremony itself is of great antiquity. Today's ritual
first took shape in the tenth century as devised by St Dunstan, Archbishop of Canterbury, for the crowning at Bath of Edgar, King of
All England and great-grandson of Alfred the Great. The present
order of service follows closely the *Liber Regalis*, written and
illuminated in the fourteenth century and one of the treasures held
by the Dean and Chapter of Westminster Abbey.

On arrival at the Abbey for her coronation in June 1953 the Queen
was received by the two Bishops whose long-established role is to
remain beside the Sovereign throughout the long ceremony (by
tradition, the Bishop of Durham and the Bishop of Bath and Wells).
The three Bishops of London, Norwich and Winchester carried the
Paten, the Bible, and the Chalice, while those who had been nominated to carry the regalia were accompanied by the Lord High
Steward bearing St Edward's Crown, by the Lord High Constable,
the Earl Marshal, the Lord Great Chamberlain, the Kings of Arms,
the Gentleman Usher of the Black Rod, and the Lord Mayor of
London. The Sovereign's Consort was accompanied by Lyon,
Scottish King of Arms, and an escort of the Gentlemen at Arms.
The Lord Chancellor, with his Pursebearer in attendance, was prominent in his ancient role as 'Keeper of the Queen's Conscience', and,
preceded by the Senior Pursuivants Bluemantle and Rouge Croix,

came four Knights of the Garter carrying the golden canopy used during the anointing. The Keeper of the Jewel House bore on a cushion the Jewelled Sword (the Sovereign's personal sword, entitled in the ritual 'the Sword of Offering'), together with the two gold bracelets known as the Armills and the Coronation Ring. The other swords used in the coronation rites are the Sword of State, the Swords of Justice to the Spirituality and Justice to the Temporality, and Curtana, or the blunt-edged Sword of Mercy.

The Queen herself walked at the end of the long procession, and among her retinue were the Master of the Horse, the Keeper of Her Majesty's Privy Purse, an escort comprising two Officers and 20 Gentlemen at Arms, and finally two Officers and 12 Yeomen of the Queen's Bodyguard of the Yeomen of the Guard. The whole procession into the Abbey was about 250 strong and comprised those of greatest distinction in this country and the Commonwealth. The Archbishop of Canterbury conducted the ceremony as was his right by ancient tradition, with the Dean of Westminster, equally by tradition, occupying the secondary role in the rites.

The coronation service began when the Queen reached the area between the Choir and the Sanctuary known as the 'Theatre' – a central space designed for the coronation ceremony in Edward the Confessor's original Minster and preserved in Henry III's rebuilding. Here are the three chairs used by the Sovereign during the ceremony: the Chair of State; the Throne, approached by five steps; and King Edward's Chair, made to the order of Edward I in 1301 and built to hold the Stone of Scone, captured from the Scots in 1296. King Edward's Chair was first used for the coronation of Edward II, first Prince of Wales, in 1308.

The coronation rites opened with the Recognition. The Queen stood in the centre of the Theatre, where all could see her, while the Archbishop pronounced the words, solemnly and resonantly, 'Sirs, I here present your undoubted Queen, wherefore all you who are come this day to do your homage and service, are you willing to do the same?' All then cried 'God Save Queen Elizabeth' and the trumpets sounded.

The Oath followed, then the Presentation of the Bible and the commencement of the Communion Service. After the Creed came the Anointing, for which the Queen, aided by the Lord Great Chamberlain, removed her crimson robe and took her place in King Edward's Chair, clad in a simple white gown and almost concealed from view by the canopy held by the Knights of the Garter. This is where two of the most ancient coronation treasures come into use – the Ampulla and the Anointing Spoon. With these the Dean of Westminster anointed the Queen – on the palms of each hand, on the breast, and on the crown of the head, a rite by which Divine confirmation is bestowed on the choice of the people. The Ampulla (basically of the fourteenth century with later work of 1661) is of gold and takes the form of an eagle, the Holy Oil being poured from the beak. The silver-gilt Anointing Spoon is attributed to the twelfth century and is believed to have been used at the coronation of King John.

Investment of the royal robes and ornaments is the next step leading to the great moment of the crowning. First the Queen was robed in a sleeveless white garment (the *Colobium Sindonis*) over which was placed a robe of cloth of gold lined with crimson silk (the *Supertunica*). The Lord Great Chamberlain then touched the Queen's hands with the Golden Spurs, symbol of chivalry; the Archbishop presented to her the Jewelled Sword, then the Armills (the golden bracelets of sovereignty and wisdom, which represent the bond uniting Sovereign and people); the Robe Royal and Stole Royal were placed upon the Queen, she was invested with the Orb and Sceptre, and the Coronation Ring was placed on the fourth finger of her right hand.

The moment of crowning had come. All in the Abbey rose and the Archbishop, having first placed St Edward's Crown on the altar for dedication, raised it on high, then solemnly lowered it on to the Queen's head. At that instant the Princes and Princesses, Peers and Peeresses, assumed their coronets, and the Kings of Arms their crowns, all acclaiming 'God Save the Queen' as trumpets sounded and the guns of the Tower of London boomed forth in Royal Salute.

Enthronement followed, for which the Queen was escorted from King Edward's Chair to take her place upon the Throne, where she received the homage of the Princes and the Peers. First came her husband, Prince Philip, Duke of Edinburgh. He removed his coronet, ascended the steps before the Throne and knelt before the Queen, placing his hands between hers and pronouncing the words of homage: 'I Philip, Duke of Edinburgh, do become your liege man of life and limb, and of earthly worship; and faith and truth I will bear unto you, to live and die, against all manner of folks. So help me God'. Then rising, he touched the crown and kissed the Queen's left cheek. The Princes of the blood followed and did likewise, and the Senior Peers in their turn paid homage, touching the crown and kissing the Queen's right hand. With the homage ended, there was the beating of drums and the sounding of trumpets, while all cried 'God save Queen Elizabeth, Long live Queen Elizabeth, May the Queen live for ever'. Simplest and most touching moment of all came towards the end of this long and solemn ceremony when the Queen and her husband knelt bareheaded before the altar to receive Holy Communion.

During the Recess in St Edward's Chapel the Queen was arrayed in her Royal Purple Robe in place of the Crimson Robe, and the weighty St Edward's Crown was replaced by the lighter Imperial State Crown. Then, with the Sceptre in her right hand and the Orb in her left, Queen Elizabeth II moved with the stately procession towards the West Door as the National Anthem rang through the Abbey and the bells pealed joyously from the bell tower.

And that, very briefly, is the ceremonial of the ancient coronation service. Never was it more graciously performed, and in the years since that June day in 1953 no monarch in the history of this country has undertaken the duties of Sovereignty with greater charm and dedication.

The Queen's Bodyguards

Among the most colourful and historic figures to play their part in royal ceremonial are the Sovereign's personal bodyguards. They consist of four Corps, all of highly honoured status. Only two, however, are applicable to this book – the Honourable Corps of Gentlemen at Arms and the Queen's Bodyguard of the Yeomen of the Guard. The other two Corps, whose duties lie outside the capital, are the Royal Company of Archers, representing the Queen's

Bodyguard for Scotland, and the Military Knights of Windsor, in the service of the Most Noble Order of the Garter (founded as the 'Poor Knights' by Edward III in 1348 and assuming the present title in the nineteenth century).

The Honourable Corps of Gentlemen at Arms

On great ceremonial occasions the Royal Bodyguard nearest to the Sovereign is the Honourable Corps of Gentlemen at Arms, senior of the four Corps but not the oldest. Now composed of retired Army Officers, the Corps was founded by Henry VIII in 1509 as a Bodyguard additional to the Yeomen of the Guard. Its members, as the title implies, were all men of gentle or noble birth, originally known as the Gentlemen Spears – a title which changed to Gentlemen Pensioners later in the sixteenth century and to the present title during the reign of William IV.

Henry VIII's reign was clouded with controversy and insecurity, and it was obvious, therefore, that he needed to be well furnished with bodyguards; and since he had a taste for spectacle and pageantry, he also required plenty of personal attendants to embellish the scene. At the historic meeting with François I on the Field of the Cloth of Gold in 1520 the Gentlemen Spears were all arrayed, by royal decree, in raiment of cloth of gold. Always, in peace or in war, this Bodyguard was at the King's side. Queen Elizabeth I had equal faith in the Corps founded by her father.

The Honourable Corps of Gentlemen at Arms remains today the Royal Bodyguard nearest to the Sovereign during all great ceremonies of state. In number the Corps consists of five Officers and 27 Gentlemen at Arms, and part of their equipment is the collection of fine ceremonial battle axes which have survived through three centuries. Their headquarters is St James's Palace.

The Queen's Bodyguard of the Yeomen of the Guard

The oldest Royal Bodyguard and the oldest military Corps in the world is the Queen's Bodyguard of the Yeomen of the Guard. The year of their foundation, 1485, was one of the most important turning points in English history for it marked the end of the Wars of the Roses, the bitter strife caused by the rival Lancastrian and Yorkist claims to the throne. The struggle lasted for nearly 30 years, but peace came to England at last with the Battle of Bosworth and the death of Richard III. Henry Tudor, Earl of Richmond and direct descendant of John of Gaunt, Duke of Lancaster, ascended the throne as Henry VII, and on his marriage with Elizabeth of York, daughter of Edward IV, the long and disastrous feud was at an end.

Although the official date of foundation of the Yeomen of the Guard was this Battle of Bosworth year of 1485, the Guard had come into being, unofficially, two years earlier. During Henry Tudor's exile in Brittany there had gathered around him a private guard of faithful and loyal followers. When he set sail for England they sailed with him, and at the ensuing Battle of Bosworth it was this private Guard who protected the future Tudor King when Richard III made his desperate personal attack upon him – the attempt to eliminate his royal enemy in which he himself was killed.

In the years and reigns that have ensued the Yeomen of the Guard have remained the Sovereign's Bodyguard. For 250 years they served as a military guard of the Sovereign's body in battle, and for a total of 300 years they shouldered the heavy responsibility, at home, of ensuring the personal safety of the Sovereign. They guarded the interior of the royal palaces and their duties included tasting the Sovereign's food and providing a member of the Guard to sleep outside the royal bedroom. A legacy of this latter duty is remembered in the initials YBG and YBH which appear against the names of certain Yeomen on the Roll. They recall the long-extinct services as Yeoman Bed-goer and Yeoman Bed-hanger; the former tested the royal bed against the danger of a weapon being hidden in the mattress, and the latter inspected the bed hangings.

The Yeomen of the Guard were with Henry VIII at the Field of the Cloth of Gold, and they were with Elizabeth I at Tilbury in 1588, prior to defeat of the Spanish Armada, when the armour-clad Queen addressed the troops with the famous words: 'I know that I have but the body of a weak and feeble woman; but I have the heart of a king, and of a king of England too, and think foul scorn that Parma, or Spain, or any prince of Europe, should dare to invade the borders of my realm'. When the monarch led his men into battle (the last King to do so was George II at the Battle of Dettingen) the Guard fought in many a famous campaign; and at home, it was the Yeomen of the Guard who arrested Guy Fawkes on 5 November 1605, thus defeating the Gunpowder Plot conspirators in their plan to blow up King James I and his Parliament.

The Tudor uniform of the Yeomen of the Guard is among the most famous and picturesque in the world. It has changed little since 1485 and consists of a full knee-length scarlet tunic with purple and gold ornamentation, scarlet knee breeches and stockings, and a round-brimmed flat-topped hat with a circlet of red, white and blue ribbon rosettes; ribbon rosettes also ornament knees and shoes. The white neck ruff was first introduced by Queen Elizabeth I but it was discarded during the Stuart period, together with the hat, in favour of lace at the neck and a plumed head-dress. The ruff was re-introduced by the Hanoverian monarchs. Earlier than this, in Queen Anne's time, the Tudor hat had been reinstated and remains to this day. The embroidered emblems on front and back of the tunic change with each reign.

The difference between the uniform of the Queen's Bodyguard of the Tower of London (who are also Yeomen of the Guard, but not members of the Queen's Bodyguard) is the gold-embroidered cross-belt worn by the former, originally used to support the butt of the heavy weapon known as an arquebus. The ceremonial pikes or halberds carried by the Yeomen of the Guard today are known as Partisans.

Early in the nineteenth century (by which time duties had become purely ceremonial) the members of the Queen's Bodyguard of the Yeomen of the Guard ceased residing in the royal palaces and were able to live in their own homes, on call for duty. Only the Senior Messenger Sergeant Major now resides at St James's Palace.

The special ceremonial occasions on which the Guard are in attendance are: the coronation or funeral of the Sovereign; the Investiture of the Prince of Wales at Caernarvon Castle and all Investitures at Buckingham Palace; the State Opening of Parliament; the offering of the Sovereign's gifts of gold, frankincense and myrrh at the Epiphany Service in the Chapel Royal of St James's Palace; the Royal Maundy Service; and the annual search of the cellars of the Houses of Parliament prior to the State Opening of Parliament.

For this last duty the Guard, equipped with lanterns, carry out a ceremonial tour of the cellars – traditionally ensuring that no twentieth-century Guy Fawkes is lurking with kegs of gunpowder beneath the Palace of Westminster when Parliament reassembles and the Queen reads the Most Gracious Speech.

The Royal Watermen

Among the most ancient appointments of the Royal Household is that of the Royal Watermen, the highest office to which any Thames Waterman can aspire, with the top rung of the ladder occupied by the Queen's Bargemaster. There are 22 Royal Watermen (with the Queen's Bargemaster, 23 in all), and their scarlet uniform is still the skirted-tunic design of the Thames Waterman of former days. With it is worn a dark blue cap, scarlet stockings, a white shirt and black tie. The gold and silver badge on the front and back of the uniform bears the national emblems – the Lion, the Thistle, the Shamrock and the Leek, and the uniform buttons bear the Royal Cypher. The uniform of the Queen's Bargemaster is of different design, with a tail-coated jacket ornamented with gold braid, and his stockings are white instead of scarlet.

Although the Royal Watermen are said to have existed from time immemorial, one story relegates their foundation to the fourteenth century. King Edward 11, so the story goes, was being ferried across the River Fleet on a dark and moonless night when he was attacked by a group of belligerent Watermen. He resolved henceforth to maintain his own trusted Watermen, and since that time they have been part of the Royal Household. Each is chosen by the Sovereign from the ranks of those Thames Watermen who have been born and bred to the life of the river, and each receives the Royal Warrant of appointment signed by the Lord Chamberlain. Most of them are top-ranking professional scullers and oarsmen – Doggett's Coat and Badge winners, boatbuilders, and scull and oar makers. A Royal Waterman who runs his own business as boatbuilder, boat-hirer, lighterman, or scull and oar maker may display the Royal Arms once on the outside of his premises.

To be appointed a Royal Waterman does not bring wealth, for

the pay is nominal, but for a Thames Waterman the honour and prestige are beyond any scale of pay. His services are only required on ceremonial occasions – for instance, for the State Opening of Parliament the Queen's Bargemaster and four Royal Watermen are always honoured with the task of guarding the Crown, which is conveyed from Buckingham Palace to Westminster in Queen Alexandra's Coach. On this day the Queen's Bargemaster and the Royal Watermen report first of all at the Royal Mews, and from here they set out with Queen Alexandra's Coach for Buckingham Palace where the Crown awaits them, having already been collected from the Tower of London. Then the coach, with a Cavalry Escort, sets out along the processional route of the Mall – about 10 to 15 minutes before the Queen herself leaves the Palace. The Queen's Bargemaster, accompanied by either one or two of the Royal Watermen, stands on the raised ledge at the rear of the coach, and this procedure is repeated for the return journey from Westminster to the Palace.

Other ceremonial occasions when the Queen's Bargemaster and the Royal Watermen are on duty are the coronation of the Sovereign, royal weddings, and State Visits of Royalty or Heads of State of other countries. They are on escort duty on the royal carriages during the State Drive of a Royal Visit, and are also on duty when the Sovereign's guests are conveyed by river, or visit places of historic Thames association, such as Greenwich or Hampton Court. They usually form the Guard of Honour when the Sovereign attends any function connected with the water – such as, for instance, the Investiture of Sir Francis Chichester at Greenwich, and the opening of the new London Bridge on 16 March 1973.

The Sovereign's Bargemaster is a prominent figure in the coronation procession, for he walks alone ahead of the Royal Watermen, only separated (at the coronation of Queen Elizabeth II) from the gold coronation coach by the Mounted Band of the Royal Horse Guards and the Sovereign's Escort. The Queen's Bargemaster was then, as he is now (in 1974) H. A. (Bert) Barry, World Professional Sculling Champion 1928–30, Doggett's Coat and Badge winner 1925, and winner of 454 races in all kinds of boats during 28 years of racing. He was appointed Royal Waterman in 1932 and became the Queen's Bargemaster in 1952 at the age of 49 – one of the youngest of the

Sovereign's Bargemasters to be appointed. His uncle, Ernest Barry, who was five times World Professional Sculling Champion and a Doggett winner, was King's Bargemaster to King George VI in 1950–51. The remarkable championship record of the Barry family is given more fully in the Doggett section (see p. 98).

To be appointed Queen's Bargemaster is an honour earned by quality and achievement. When the Queen's Bargemaster rides by, standing behind one of the royal carriages during a State Drive (as do the other Royal Watermen) this is not merely a royal postilion in livery who is seen, but a champion of the river.

The Royal Maundy

Distribution of the Royal Maundy is one of the most ancient ceremonies in Britain. It takes place each year on Maundy Thursday (the Thursday before Easter) when the specially minted Maundy money is handed to recipients numbering as many men and as many women as the Sovereign has years. The origin of the Maundy ceremony was the Last Supper, when Jesus, as recorded by St John, 'riseth from supper and laid aside His garments; and took a towel and girded Himself. After that He poureth water into a basin, and began to wash the Disciples' feet and to wipe them with the towel wherewith he was girded'.

It is the command (or *mandatum*) of Jesus, to 'Do as I have done to you' that each Maundy ceremony is fulfilling, and from this word the title is believed to derive. Another theory has been expressed that the title came from the Saxon word *mand*, which developed into *maund*, meaning a basket, and this was the word used in early days for any gift or alms so carried.

The ceremony has long been an ecclesiastical rite in Christian churches of many lands, but in this country it was an act of royal humility as early as the twelfth century. Henry I's Queen – known as Good Queen Maud owing to her great piety – came bare-footed and bare-legged to Westminster Abbey during Lent, and on Maundy Thursday she washed and kissed the feet of the poor. One courtier took exception to this act of humility, as related in the Chronicle of Robert of Gloucester:

'Madame, for Goddes love is this well idoo
To handle such unclene lymmes, and to kiss so;
Foule wolde the Kynge thynk if that he wiste,
And ryght wel avyle hym or he your mouth kiste!'
'Sur, Sur' sd. the Quene, 'be stille; why sayst thou so?
Our Lord hymself ensamble gaf so for to do'.

In 1213 King John performed the Maundy ceremony at Rochester, distributing 13 pence to 13 men, and from the reign of his grandson, Edward I, there are continuous records of royal participation in the Maundy Thursday ritual. In 1556 Queen Mary I took special pains to ensure that her gown was well bestowed. She progressed the whole length of the hall upon her knees, washing the feet of the poor and finally selecting the oldest and poorest woman present as the recipient of her gown.

Her sister, Queen Elizabeth I, blended humility with fastidiousness. In 1572 she performed the ceremony at the Palace of Greenwich where, attended by 39 ladies and gentlemen of the Court, she distributed the Royal Maundy to 39 poor men and 39 poor women. Unlike Good Queen Maud – and the equally devout but certainly less good Queen Mary – she organised preparatory washing before her own turn came. First of all the feet of the poor were cleansed by the Yeomen of the laundry in warm water sweetened with herbs and flowers. After this ablutions were undertaken by the Sub-Almoner and the Lord High Almoner. Only then did Queen Elizabeth kneel to wash each foot, marking it with the sign of the cross, and kissing it. Queen Elizabeth I also refrained from presenting the royal gown; instead she made a gift of money, to be divided equally and amounting to 20 shillings apiece – in this she followed the example of her brother, the young King Edward VI, who ransomed his clothing for 20 shillings.

It was an outbreak of the plague which caused King Charles I to discontinue the rite of washing and kissing the feet, but on the Restoration of the Monarchy in 1660 his son, Charles II, reverted to the full 'personal service' ceremonial, as did his brother and successor, James II. William III was the last monarch to carry out this ritual in its full humility. The custom of regulating the number of

7 *The Ceremony of the Keys at the Tower of London, a 700-year-old custom which represents the locking of the Tower for the night. The Chief Yeoman Warder and escort join the main Guard who await them on the steps by the Jewel House.*

Maundy recipients to coincide with the age of the monarch dates back to the reign of Henry IV (1399–1413).

The Maundy food and clothing allocations of the past were lavish if the list of goods presented in 1731 can be regarded as typical. The distribution (in the Banqueting House, Whitehall) was to 48 men and 48 women, who received boiled beef, shoulders of mutton, ling and dried cod, 12 red herrings and 12 white herrings, bowls of ale, four quartern loaves, linen and woollen cloth, shoes and stockings, pieces of silver to the value of one, two, three and four pennies, together with shillings, amounting in all to about £4. On this occasion the Archbishop of York and the Lord High Almoner represented the monarch for the feet-washing ritual. This ritual was discontinued shortly afterwards. The distribution of food and clothing continued until the nineteenth century when it was realised that the Maundy recipients would find money gifts more beneficial.

For two centuries the Maundy ceremony took place without the personal attendance of the monarch, and only in 1932 did King George V revive the custom of royal attendance. King Edward VIII personally distributed the Royal Maundy during his short reign, and King George VI did so seven times; but it is Queen Elizabeth II who has shown especial interest in the ceremony. She has distributed the Royal Maundy in person on almost every occasion since ascending the throne, and has introduced a sense of widespread participation by varying the location of the ceremony. In early times it was carried out wherever the monarch happened to be in residence. Later, for many centuries, the venue was London – in Greenwich Palace, the Banqueting House, the old Chapel Royal in Whitehall, and, from 1890, in Westminster Abbey or, in coronation years, in St Paul's Cathedral. During the present reign the Royal Maundy has usually been distributed in Westminster Abbey in alternate years, but there is no firm ruling about this; at other times the venue has been cathedrals or churches throughout the country.

Although the feet-washing ritual was discontinued in the eighteenth century, much remains unchanged in this ancient ceremony. The Lord High Almoner and his assistants (the Sub-Almoner, together with the Secretary and Assistant Secretary of the Royal

8 (above) Swan-upping. 9 (below) The Five Bargemasters, when this group included three noted families of the river. l. to r., Michael Turk (Vintners), Harry Phelps (Fishmongers), H. A. (Bert) Barry (Queen's Bargemaster), Tom Phelps (Watermen & Lightermen), Harold Cobb (Dyers).

Almonry) are still girded with linen towels – a symbolic reminder of the towel used by Jesus to wash the feet of the Disciples on the Thursday of the first Holy Week of all. The towels now in use date back to 1883; before this, they were included each year in the clothing distribution. The custom of carrying nosegays in the Royal Maundy procession survives from the days of the plague, and these are composed of spring flowers and herbs, including daffodils, violets, primroses, rosemary and thyme. The Queen's Bodyguard of the Yeomen of the Guard lends colour and picturesqueness to the scene, and it is on one of the Yeomen's flat-topped Tudor hats that the great silver-gilt Maundy dish, bearing the purses for the first distribution, is carried up the nave to the sanctuary. This dish dates from the reign of King Charles II, as do the two altar dishes used for the second distribution. The two distributions take place at different times during the Maundy service; while anthems are sung the same recipients receive their first and second allocation of gifts directly from the Queen.

The first distribution of the Royal Maundy money is in green purses handed to the women and white purses to the men; these are in lieu of the former presentation of clothing. The contents of the red purses of the second distribution represent money in lieu of food and the royal gown, while the white purses contain the specially minted silver Maundy money in one, two, three and four penny coins. Their total value is as many pence as the years of age of the Queen. In decimal currency the set of four coins is equivalent to 10 new pence, and they can be used as money – although few Maundy recipients ever cash the Maundy coins, for these almost invariably become treasured possessions.

The Choir of the Chapel Royal, clad in their traditional gold-braided red tunics, play an important role in the Royal Maundy ceremony. This Choir's history is long and notable, for in past days they accompanied the monarch on his or her travels in war and in peace. Two historic occasions when the Choir of the Chapel Royal sang were on Henry V's victory at the Battle of Agincourt (1415) and at that most magnificent of all royal spectacles, the meeting between Henry VIII and François I of France on the Field of the Cloth of Gold (1520).

Queen Elizabeth II's participation in this Royal Maundy ceremony is very personal, and as she walks along the lines of recipients during the first and second distributions it is very evident that both the ceremony and the recipients are of the greatest interest to her. Until recent years the Maundy beneficiaries were, once chosen, able to receive the Maundy money every year for the rest of their lives. This ruling is now changed, mainly owing to the varying cities in which the ceremony is held, and a new list of recipients is prepared each year. They are always elderly but the qualification is no longer extreme poverty; it is, instead, a record of service to the Church and to the community which is being recognised. A qualification of hardship does, however, apply to four participants in the ceremony – the Maundy children, two boys and two girls, usually orphans or children of a widowed mother. They walk in the procession, carrying nosegays, and they receive the Maundy money, a contribution also being made to the mother or guardian.

The Royal Maundy ceremony is a memorable experience – to see the Yeomen of the Guard lining the nave of Westminster Abbey and the massive Maundy Dish carried on the head of its Yeoman bearer, to see the graciousness with which the Queen carries out the two distributions, and to hear the fine singing of the Choir of the Chapel Royal, is somehing likely to linger in the mind for a lifetime. To receive the purses is more memorable still.

The Queen's Gifts on the Feast of the Epiphany

The Chapel Royal, St James's Palace. 6 January

In the Gospel of St Matthew the tale is told of the journey of the Magi, the Wise Men of the East, who came to Jerusalem in search of the Holy Child and were guided by a star which, moving ahead, led them to the stable of the Nativity in Bethlehem. On Twelfth Day, 6 January, this journey of the Magi with gifts of gold, frankincense and myrrh, is remembered in all Christian churches, but nowhere is the Feast of the Epiphany celebrated more picturesquely and with greater tradition than in the Chapel Royal of St James's Palace.

For a period now approaching 900 years this Epiphany Service has re-enacted the offerings of the Magi in the Sovereign's presentation of gold, frankincense and myrrh. Until the second half of the eighteenth century the Sovereign carried out the ceremony in person, but the illness of George III established the custom of representation – today by two Gentlemen Ushers of the Household wearing full Service Dress. The ceremony takes place in every way as if the Queen herself were making the presentation, the two Gentlemen Ushers arriving by royal limousine through the Great Gates of St James's Palace and being escorted to the Royal Pew (a gallery over the west door).

The scene in the Chapel Royal for the Epiphany Service is truly impressive. The Queen's Bodyguard of the Yeomen of the Guard, in the full splendour of their Tudor uniform, line the aisle; the choristers – who bear the traditional title of the Gentlemen and Children of the Chapel Royal – provide another splash of colour, with the boys in their gold-braided scarlet tunics; and gleaming on the altar is the massed array of the Chapel Royal's seventeenth-century Sacramental plate. The Bishop of London, as Dean of Her Majesty's Chapels Royal, receives and dedicates the offerings.

The Epiphany Service opens with the procession of the choir and clergy followed by a detachment of the Yeomen of the Guard, and the National Anthem is sung. The Holy Communion service then commences, and after the Creed an appropriate Anthem (often *The Three Kings* by Cornelius) indicates that the moment has come for the presentation of the offerings. From the west door the Serjeant of the Vestry, bearing his silver-gilt wand, leads to the altar the two Gentlemen Ushers. They carry, on two silver-gilt salvers, the traditional gifts of gold, frankincense and myrrh. Behind them comes the escort, composed of the Serjeant-Major and two Yeomen of the Guard, and three times the little procession stops for the Gentlemen Ushers to bow to the altar. These offerings, received by the Dean of the Chapels Royal on one of the Chapel's great almsdishes, are then dedicated and laid reverently upon the altar. The representatives of the Queen retire, again turning and bowing, and the offertory hymn follows. At the close of the hymn the Yeomen of the Guard retire and the Communion service continues.

The frankincense and myrrh for this royal Epiphany Service are still supplied, as in the past, by the Apothecary to the Household; the gold, which until the reign of Queen Victoria was a roll of gold leaf, was replaced in 1860 by 25 new sovereigns on the wish of the Prince Consort that the offering could be put to charitable use. Today 25 sovereigns are offered, their value later being exchanged for present-day currency and used for charity.

The Wise Men of the East have been given various attributions through the centuries, for in the scriptures neither their number nor their names are given. Only in the legends which gathered around the tale of their star-guided journey to Bethlehem were they numbered as three and elevated to the status of Kings. A variety of names was allocated to them, but most generally they are known as the Kings Caspar, Melchior and Balthazar. Caspar, according to legend, was King of Tarshish; Melchior was King of Nubia; and Balthazar was King of Chaldea. Tradition says that they were baptised by St Thomas and devoted the rest of their lives to preaching the Gospel. It is also said that the Empress Helena, mother of Constantine the Great, found the place of burial of the Three Kings and brought their bodies to Constantinople, whence they were later transferred to Milan. In 1164 the Emperor Frederick I (Barbarossa), following his successful siege of Milan, presented the bodies to the Archbishop of Cologne. Here their shrine, richly embellished with gold and precious stones, became one of the great centres of pilgrimage of medieval times. The shrine, despite the bombs and destruction of the last war, has survived in Cologne Cathedral to this day.

The Chapel Royal of St James's Palace dates from 1540, and its elaborate ceiling, believed to have been designed by Holbein, displays the entwined initials of Henry VIII and his fourth Queen, Anne of Cleves (from whom he succeeded in disentwining himself very speedily). The later section of the ceiling at the western end dates from 1837 and bears the initials of William IV and Queen Adelaide. It was in this Chapel, on 30 January 1649, that King Charles I received the Sacrament before his execution; and here, on 10 February 1840, the marriage of Queen Victoria and the Prince Consort was solemnised. It is a Chapel which has witnessed scenes of royal joy and sadness, and owing to its smallness it lends a special sense of intimacy to the dignity of this historic royal Epiphany Service.

The Tower of London

It is obvious that any structure so ancient and steeped in history as the Tower of London will have accumulated old customs and ceremonies. Since the eleventh century the Tower has dominated the River Thames from the eastern fringe of the old City wall, for the White Tower (the great central Keep) was built by Gundulph for William I following the Conquest. It served two purposes – as a fortress to protect the City of London from outside attack, and as a fortified residence for the Norman King himself. As the centuries rolled by the rest of the buildings of this fortress community came into being. Today the Tower of London stands partly within the City boundaries and partly without, yet it remains a place apart, a Liberty in its own right. It is responsible for the custody of the Crown Jewels, and from the time of the Conquest until the early years of the nineteenth century the Royal Mint was housed within its walls.

Many a life came to an untimely end on Tower Green and Tower Hill, and murder, too, played its part in the record. In 1471 King Henry VI was murdered within the Tower walls, and in 1483 the little Princes of the Tower (Edward V and his brother, Richard Duke of York) were mysteriously murdered and buried within the Tower. On Tower Green Queen Anne Boleyn, Queen Catherine Howard, and the Nine-Days-Queen, Lady Jane Grey, were beheaded; and within the Tower Sir Thomas More, Sir Walter Raleigh, Robert Devereux Earl of Essex, and the Gunpowder Plotter Guy Fawkes, all suffered imprisonment prior to execution. But this is to mention only a small number of the famous prisoners whose days drew to a close in the Tower of London.

The Tower remained a royal palace and home up to the reign of James I. As a State Prison it received its last political prisoner in 1820 – although later it was used to house Prisoners of War, including Rudolf Hess in 1941.

Among the old customs which have survived the passing of the centuries, the Tudor uniform of the Yeomen Warders is one of the most picturesque symbols of unchanging tradition. It would be unheard of to modernise this famous uniform of the custodians of the

Tower. Their State Dress is a red and gold tunic with white ruff at the neck and flat-topped head-dress (known as a Tudor bonnet), almost identical to the uniform of the Queen's Bodyguard of the Yeomen of the Guard, except for absence of the crossbelt (see p. 64). Their undress uniform, more practical but also picturesque, consists of a ruffless dark blue tunic with scarlet ornamentation. The Yeomen Warders bear the title 'Yeomen of the Guard Extraordinary' and they are composed of ex-military personnel. Their appointment, until retirement at the age of 65, is full-time duty at the Tower of London.

On ceremonial occasions the Chief Yeoman Warder at the Tower carries a mace surmounted by a silver replica of the White Tower, and the Yeoman Gaoler (his second-in-command) carries the ceremonial axe. This axe dates from the reign of Henry VII but is not, as some people imagine, the execution axe. It was always carried in front of prisoners on their journey from the Tower to trial at Westminster, and one glance at the axe, when the prisoner emerged after the trial, conveyed the verdict; if the sharp edge pointed towards him he was guilty, and if pointed away, not guilty. The mace dates from 1792 and was originally the Coroner's mace when the Coroner's Court sat in the Tower of London. On ceremonial occasions the Yeomen Warders (other than the Chief Warder and the Yeoman Gaoler) carry the same halberd or pike/partisan as that borne by the Queen's Bodyguard of the Yeomen of the Guard.

Unless special events warrant it, the State Dress of the Yeomen Warders is only worn three times a year: for the Church Parade on Easter Sunday, Whit Sunday and the Sunday before Christmas Day, when the Yeomen Warders form an escort for the Resident Governor; otherwise it is worn in the presence of Royalty and at the installation of the Constable of the Tower. Exception is made, however, if a Yeoman Warder is married while serving in the Tower; then, by the Resident Governor's permission, he may have an escort of Yeomen Warders in State Dress. This also applies on the marriage of a son or daughter of a serving Yeoman Warder. State Dress is worn for Beating the Bounds.

The most famous and oldest of the Tower's customs is the Ceremony of the Keys, a short but impressive ceremony which has been carried out with little change for about 700 years. It represents the official locking of the Tower for the night. In very early days it was the duty of the locksmith to close and lock the gates, but it soon became apparent that he needed a military escort, and the duty was transferred to the Yeoman Warder, known originally as the Gentleman Porter or Yeoman Porter. The locking of the Tower was of vital importance for here were guarded the Crown Jewels; also, when the Royal Mint was housed within the Tower, much gold, silver and copper was stored within the walls, together with arms and ammunition. Today up-to-date equipment serves as protection for the Tower, but the Ceremony of the Keys still continues and is a tradition unlikely to be broken.

For the Ceremony of the Keys an escort of three Guardsmen together with the Sergeant of the Guard forms up under the archway of the Bloody Tower. Three members of the Guard are armed with rifles, the remaining Guardsman being unarmed as he will carry the lantern. The Chief Yeoman Warder (or the Yeoman Gaoler if he is undertaking the duty) leaves the Byward Tower with his lantern and the Keys at seven minutes before 10 pm (21.53). He joins the escort and hands over the lantern, takes up his position between two front Guardsmen, and they march to the farthest gate, the West Gate. On arrival, the Sergeant halts the escort and they present arms, which represents a salute to the Keys while the gates are being locked (throughout, the Keys themselves are an important part of the ceremony, as representing Her Majesty the Queen). The same procedure is carried out on the return, both at the Middle Tower and the Byward Tower. On approaching the Bloody Tower archway the sentry cries 'Halt!' The escort under the command of the Sergeant obeys, and the sentry calls, 'Who goes there?'

'The Keys,' answers the Chief Warder.

'Whose Keys?' asks the sentry.

'Queen Elizabeth's Keys' is the reply.

The sentry then allows the escort to pass, and they march to join the main Guard, who are awaiting their return on the broad steps in front of the Jewel House. The Officer in Charge commands the whole Guard and escort to present arms, and then the Chief Warder steps forward, raises his Tudor bonnet on high and cries, 'God preserve Queen Elizabeth'. The Guard respond 'Amen', and these final words coincide with the first stroke of the clock as it tolls the hour of 10 pm and a bugler sounds the Last Post. The Chief Warder then collects the lantern from the Guardsman and makes his way to the Queen's House, where he hands over the Keys to the Resident Governor for safe keeping until the morning. There used to be a morning ceremony for the unlocking of the Tower, but this was discontinued in 1913.

Beating the Bounds is undertaken at the Tower on Ascension Day once every three years. This custom, of Saxon origin, used to take place widely throughout the country and was a means of protecting ownership of boundaries. Today the Port of London Authority has built on part of the territory of the Tower Liberty, and it is necessary to enter PLA land in order to complete the beating of the boundary stones. There are 29 in all, between the jetty of the Port of London Authority to the west and the old stone jetty beneath Tower Bridge to the east.

Beating the Bounds at the Tower starts with a short service in the Chapel Royal of St Peter ad Vincula. Afterwards each choirboy is issued with a willow wand and then, accompanied by the Chief Warder and the Chaplain of the Tower, they set out on their tour of the boundary stones. At each stone the Chaplain announces, 'Cursed is he who removeth his neighbours' landmark', and then the Chief Warder gives the command, 'Whack it, boys, whack it!' The boys whack with a will until the Chief Warder stops them – which is necessary fairly soon in the early stages of the Beating or little of the willow wands would survive for the later stones. Finally all return to the Tower and, after singing the National Anthem, they dismiss.

On 21 May each year a ceremony takes place in the Tower which recalls the good deeds of a sad King. The Wakefield Tower is where, in a small oratory, Henry VI is believed to have been murdered in 1471, and each year, on the anniversary of his death, flowers are placed on the spot where, traditionally, he was struck down – white lilies from Eton College and white roses from King's College, Cambridge, both of which he founded.

The Tower ravens represent a firmly established custom, and six of these large, black and rather sinister birds are officially part of the Tower community. They strut on Tower Green with an air of evil intent and confidence in their indispensability – well justified, in fact, for the ravens are considered essential to the wellbeing of the Tower and the country. This superstition had its origin, it is believed, in the early years of Charles ii's reign – that should the Tower ravens become extinct the White Tower would fall and the British Empire disintegrate. The White Tower still stands as firmly as ever it did, the British Empire has transformed itself through the looser ties of the British Commonwealth of Nations – and the ravens strut on, confident and unlikeable. They qualify for a ration allowance, contributed for their upkeep by the Government.

Ravens have been at the Tower, it seems, ever since the Norman Conquest brought the stronghold into being. They came to London from the marshland of Essex, attracted by foodscraps and also, doubt-less, the possibility of capturing mice and rats. Ravens are carrion eaters, and they nest in trees and high rocky places; therefore they chose the turrets of the White Tower, of exceptional height, as their nesting place. This continued over a long period and no one challenged their occupancy until an enemy appeared in the form of the first Astronomer Royal, John Flamsteed, who selected the roof of the White Tower for his observations some time between 1672 and 1674. The raucous cries of the ravens so exasperated the Astronomer Royal that he requested their removal; and that, in view of the superstition, posed a problem indeed. A compromise was sought, and six only of the ravens were retained while the rest were removed.

The official roll of ravens at the Tower remains six, although at the time of writing there are also a couple of 'guest ravens'. All have the freedom of the grounds, but they cannot fly away for their wings are clipped.

The Tower ravens have a Yeoman Warder, known as the Raven Master, delegated to their care. His duty is to feed them, clean the cage where they sleep, and see that they are all safely locked up in their cage for the night. It would seem that the nightly task of coaxing these obstinate birds into their cage might take some doing, but there is, apparently, no difficulty at all; as soon as dusk falls, the ravens begin to make their way to the cage of their own accord.

The names on the present roll of Tower ravens are: Merry, Hectora, Garvey, Kala 2, Grog, and Brorai; they hail from North and South Wales, Sutherland, the Isle of Man and Cornwall. The two guest ravens are Larry and George, both from North Wales. With the full complement of six ravens and two guest ravens as 'reserves', the legendary calamity should be held safely at bay.

Beating the Bounds of the Manor of the Savoy

Ascension Day – approximately every five years

At about five-yearly intervals, on Ascension Day, the ceremony of Beating the Bounds of the Manor of the Savoy is undertaken by the choirboys of the Queen's Chapel of the Savoy. This is a custom similar in origin and practice to the Beating the Bounds ceremony at the Tower of London – but where are the boundaries of the Manor of the Savoy? Few people, if asked casually, can answer this question, yet the Manor covers an area of London much frequented by Londoners and visitors, most of whom fail to notice the occasional cast iron boundary mark which bears the emblem of the Duchy of Lancaster.

The Manor of the Savoy is land possessing an ancient Liberty of 700 years' standing, and it was, until comparatively recent times, responsible for its own independent government in local affairs. The governing body was the Court Leet, and in the Duchy of Lancaster Office are still preserved the weights and measures of the Savoy Liberty whereby it was ensured that the shops within the Liberty were giving good measure in their trading. The Liberty had its own Constables for maintaining the peace, and their distinctive batons are still held at the Duchy office. Today all such matters are handled by central government. In 1863 the Constables, Aleconners and Flesh-tasters had their appointments cancelled and the offices abolished, so that by the end of the nineteenth century the duties of the Court were limited to perambulation of the Liberty for Beating the Bounds.

Within the boundaries of the Manor of the Savoy lie Somerset

House, part of London University, a stretch of the Thames Embankment, part of the parishes of St Clement Danes and St Mary-le-Strand, hotels (including the famous Savoy Hotel), and a whole multitude of shops. Part of the Strand falls within the boundaries, and in early times this was just what its name implies – the foreshore which sloped down to the northern bank of the Thames. This whole territory, so densely built upon today and so seasoned to the roar of traffic, was once open land through which a thicket-bordered road linked Westminster with the City of London. It belonged to neither.

No records survive to prove when this area became a Liberty. In 1246 it was granted by Henry III to Peter, Count of Savoy (uncle of his Queen, Eleanor of Provence). Peter of Savoy was one of the Queen's many kinsmen on whom Henry III bestowed land and position in such profusion that he aroused the smouldering discontent of his people, and Queen Eleanor, though beloved by her husband, became one of the least-loved of England's Queens. Thus Peter of Savoy, a nobleman from beyond these shores, gave his name to an area which is as typically British as any in the land. After 1263 he returned to the ancestral estates of the Counts of Savoy, and in the course of time the English property passed to Henry III's son Edmund, first Earl of Lancaster. The Manor continued to be held by the family of Lancaster until, in the time of John of Gaunt, his Palace of the Savoy was deemed the most splendid in the land, magnificent in structure and filled with treasures. In 1381 all was lost, palace and contents, in Wat Tyler's revolt.

The palace ruins remained for a considerable time, but as a palace they never rose again. At the beginning of the sixteenth century Henry VII set about founding on the site a royal hostel known as the Savoy Hospital – for pilgrims, strangers and sick persons. But with Henry VIII's Dissolution of the Monasteries the pilgrims came no more, and the Hospital became the haunt of vagrants loth to work – a disreputable crowd for whom the Hospital's provision of hot baths and two ovens for delousing clothing probably offered a much-needed amenity. The Hospital was finally dissolved in 1702.

The Queen's Chapel of the Savoy survives from the Savoy Hospital, of which it was the principal chapel. It was never the chapel of John of Gaunt's Palace of the Savoy. Fire, war damage, and much alteration have afflicted it at various times, but the north, west and east walls are original. It is the Chapel of the Royal Victorian Order, and as a private chapel of the Queen it is exempt from all ecclesiastical jurisdiction, coming under the sway of neither the Bishop of London nor the Archbishop of Canterbury. A tradition which prevails at the Savoy Chapel is that the National Anthem is sung in a completely distinctive style, the words being, 'God save our gracious Queen, Long live our noble Duke, God save the Queen'. The Queen, in right of the Duchy of Lancaster is Lady of the Manor of the Savoy. She is *not* the Duchess of Lancaster.

Before Beating the Bounds takes place a preliminary meeting of the Court Leet is called. The Jurymen present themselves at the Duchy of Lancaster Office (which overlooks the Thames, on the north side of Waterloo Bridge) and the Bailiff of the Liberty introduces them to the High Steward. Then the Beadle opens the proceedings with the words:

'Oyez, Oyez, Oyez. All manner of persons that do owe suit and service to this Court Leet of our Sovereign Lady the Queen now to be holden in and for this Manor of the Savoy draw near and give your Attendance'.

After the Jury have been named, the Bailiff addresses their Foreman:

'You, as Foreman of this Jury, shall enquire and true Presentment make of all such Things as shall be given you in Charge. The Queen's Counsel, your own, and your Fellows, you shall well and truly keep: you shall present nothing out of Hatred or Malice, nor shall conceal any Thing out of Love, Fear or Affection; but in all Things you shall well and truly present as the same shall come to your knowledge. So help you God'.

The Swearing then takes place, and the High Steward charges the Jury to traverse the boundaries of Her Majesty's Liberty and Manor of the Savoy. But first of all there is a short service in the Queen's Chapel, and then the procession, including the Chapel choirboys, sets out for the first of the boundary marks. Throughout the perambulation the choirboys are bumped (held upside down and literally bumped on a hassock) at a selected number of the boundary points. The marks are now more widely spaced than they used to be, for in 1810 there were 24 cast iron Duchy of Lancaster marks and today there are only 12. They are affixed at the following points:

1 Burleigh Street (on rear wall of the Lyceum Theatre).
2 Lyceum Theatre.
3 85 Strand.
4 Embankment (N.E. of Cleopatra's Needle).
5 Embankment.
6 Temple Gardens.
7 New Court.
8 Devereux Court.
9 231 Strand.
10 Strand (back wall of Child's Bank – not accessible to the general public).
11 Strand Lane.
12 Embankment (Waterloo Bridge, west side of east steps).

The purpose of Beating the Bounds has always been twofold – to establish the boundary points and also to ensure that the marks are visible and in good condition.

The cast iron boundary marks of the Manor of the Savoy can be recognised by three lions passant with a label of three points, the emblem surmounted by a crown and encircled by the words 'Duchy of Lancaster'.

CHAPTER THREE

Customs of London's River

The River Thames was, until road and rail travel competed, the undisputed highway of London. The river was alive with boats – with the Watermen's wherries (the equivalent of today's taxis) and on special occasions with the ceremonial barges which, in addition to the Royal Barge, belonged to the City Corporation, the Admiralty, and the City Livery Companies. For great occasions such as a coronation, a royal marriage, or the Lord Mayor's Day procession, the splendour of the river scene between Greenwich, the Tower of London and Westminster was something unlikely to be seen again on London's river.

Among the Thames water pageants which left their mark on history was the celebration, in 1533, of the coronation of Henry VIII's second Queen, Anne Boleyn. On her day of triumph Anne Boleyn was conveyed from Greenwich in a river procession of great splendour. Later, to mark the christening of their daughter, the future Queen Elizabeth I, a second water pageant was staged – which is somewhat surprising in view of Henry VIII's disappointment at the continued absence of a male heir. Neither he nor any of those taking part in the river celebrations could have guessed that this small and unwanted example of femininity would become one of England's greatest monarchs.

A later river pageant on a splendid scale marked the reception, in 1662, of Charles II's Portuguese bride, Catherine of Braganza. She, like Anne Boleyn, was destined to fail in the royal matrimonial duty of producing a male heir. In fact, she produced no heir at all, and was to suffer the mortification of having Charles II's mistresses flaunted before her eyes. Grand river pageants did not augur well for these two royal brides of the sixteenth and seventeenth centuries.

In the Barge House of the National Maritime Museum at Greenwich it is possible to view some of the ceremonial barges and wherries of past days. Here, for instance, is the Royal State Barge, *Queen Mary's Shallop*, built in 1689 by William III for Queen Mary II and last used during the Peace Pageant of August 1919. Even more splendid is the State Barge built in 1731–32 for Frederick, Prince of Wales. Designed by William Kent, it has gloriously rich ornamentation, with fine animal heads carved and gilded by James Richards, successor to Grinling Gibbons as Master Carver to the Crown. When Prince Frederick died in 1751 this became the principal Royal Barge (*Shallop* then rating second in importance), and it was last used to convey the Prince Consort to the City in 1849 to open the Coal Exchange.

Nowhere in London is there an actual survivor of the grand Livery Company barges of former days, but at Greenwich there is an enchanting little model of the eighteenth-century ceremonial barge of the Shipwrights' Company. Noah's Ark is its theme (the motto of the Company being 'Within the Ark Safe for Ever') and on the roof of the cabin the gilded animal figures march along, two by two. It is a sad loss that these splendid barges of the Livery Companies cannot enliven London's river scene on special occasions today, but one or two of the gilded statues of Patron Saints which once adorned the barges are given honoured places in the Companies' Halls. In Fishmongers' Hall, for instance, stands the figure of St Peter, grasping his keys as firmly as ever and gazing horizonwards as if still on the Fishmongers' barge; in Goldsmiths' Hall the gilded St Dunstan dominates the main staircase – a place of distinction certainly, but not, one feels, to his liking after the fresh breezes and open vistas of the river. The Stationers' barge was a magnificent affair, as is seen in the enlarged engraving on the Barge House wall at Greenwich; there is a small model of the barge in the entrance hall of the Stationers' Company.

The Greenwich Barge House also has examples of the old-time wherries – long, narrow and shallow in build – in which the Watermen plied for hire from the riverside stairs. The Watermen wore a

10   *Changing the Guard. The Life Guards, first in order of precedence in the British Army, set out along the Mall for the Changing the Guard ceremony at Horse Guards, Whitehall.*

11   *Searching the Cellars. The Queen's Bodyguard of the Yeomen of the Guard, lantern in hand, embark upon the traditional search of the cellars of the Palace of Westminster before the State Opening of Parliament.*

scarlet knee-length skirted-tunic uniform (one is displayed in the Barge House), and if privately employed by noble or wealthy families, the City Corporation, or the Livery Companies, they wore a silver badge on the arm which bore the employer's coat of arms. This same style of uniform is worn today by winners of Doggett's Coat and Badge Race, the famous sculling contest for Thames Watermen.

The office of Bargemaster still exists in five instances – the Queen's Bargemaster, and the Bargemasters of the four City Companies most closely associated with the river: the Fishmongers, the Vintners, the Dyers, and the Watermen and Lightermen.

Swan Upping

River Thames – Temple Stairs to Henley (6 days in July)

The swan which floats so elegantly upon the rivers of this country is the Mute Swan, white of plumage and orange of bill, with a black patch at the base of the bill. As long as records exist it has been regarded as a royal bird, although since medieval times the swans on the open Thames have had three owners – the Sovereign and two of the City Livery Companies, the Vintners and the Dyers. These two Livery Companies have what is known as a royalty of swans – a privilege which extends back, it is believed, over 600 years, although the exact date when the royal grant was made is not recorded. The Thames swans have always been protected birds, and to kill one was a crime which once earned dire punishment. As late as the mid-nineteenth century transportation for seven years was the penalty, and in 1895 it was seven weeks' hard labour.

Ownership of the Thames swans is established each year during the Swan Upping when counting, marking and pinioning of the cygnets takes place. For this task the three respective Swan Herdsmen and their teams of Swan Uppers set out each July on a week-long Swan Voyage from Temple Stairs to Henley. The distinguishing marks are one nick in the upper beak of the Dyers' swans, two nicks for those of the Vintners; the Queen's swans remain unmarked. The Swan Herdsmen at the time of writing are: John Turk, the

Queen's Swan Keeper; Michael Turk, the Vintners' Swan Marker and Bargemaster; and Harold Cobb, the Dyers' Bargemaster. There are strong hereditary links and inherited skills in these ancient river appointments. For instance, Michael Turk's father, Richard Turk, was the Vintners' Swan Marker for over 60 years. John Turk succeeded his father Fred (brother of Richard) who, after being the Dyers' Bargemaster and Swan Herdsman was appointed the Queen's Swan Keeper, whereupon a third brother, Herbert, succeeded to the Dyers' appointment. Thus, at one time, three Turk brothers held the three offices.

The name Swan Upping is believed to stem from the fact that the birds must be taken up out of the water for identification and marking; at the same time the cygnets are pinioned (wings clipped, so that they cannot attain great heights or long distances). The Vintners' accounts show that in 1563 their Swan Uppers were paid ten shillings for the Swan Voyage with ten shillings for lodging. The costs must be very different today. Apart from the fact that this is a serious job which requires great skill in handling the birds, the Swan Upping is a unique and picturesque event. It is a grand sight to see the boats come into view on the Thames with their Swan Uppers rowing sturdily and the colourful banners of the Queen and the Companies flying from each boat.

In the sixteenth and seventeenth centuries the Swan Voyage was a purely practical affair. It was in the eighteenth century that a festive element was introduced. Guests accompanied the Liverymen in the Companies' state barges, musicians were engaged to play during the voyage, guns were fired in celebration, and a vast amount of food and drink was disposed of. As the nineteenth century progressed the mood changed, for the state barges disappeared from the scene. But a festive atmosphere still prevails today as accompaniment to the sheer hard work of rowing, catching the swans and cygnets, marking and pinioning; and on two days of the Swan Voyage the Court of each of the Livery Companies, together with their guests, follow by launch in the wake of the Swan Uppers.

Towards the end of the year a Swan Feast is held in Vintners' Hall, and this is when cygnet is eaten. A fanfare from the Minstrel's Gallery heralds the ceremonial and then the Swan Procession enters, to the accompaniment of the old English melody of *Greensleeves*, played by a military band. The Swan Procession includes two Swan Uppers with their swan hooks, the Bargemaster, the Chef, the Beadle, the Stavesmen, and the Swan Warden, while the Banner of the Company is carried in the rear. On a silver dish the Chef bears a stuffed white swan (not stuffed edibly – the result of the taxidermist's art), and then the Swan Warden doffs his Elizabethan cap to the Master, saying 'Master, I present cygnets for the delectation of your guests'. The Master replies, 'Let them be served, Mr Swan'. During the Swan Feast (as during other Vintners' Company celebrations) the *Song of the Vintners* is rendered with great verve by one and all, and the first verse and chorus runs as follows:

> *Come, come, let us drink to the Vintners' good Health,*
> *'Tis the Cask, not the Coffer, that holds the true Wealth.*
> *If to founders of Blessings we Pyramids raise,*
> *The Bowl next the Sceptre deserves the best Praise.*
> *Then next to the Queen let the Vintners' Fame shine;*
> *She gives us good Laws and they fill us good Wine.*

> Chorus:
> *Come, come, let us drink to the Vintners' good Health,*
> *'Tis the Cask, not the Coffer, that holds the true Wealth.*

After the Vintners' Song comes the toast, and this commemorates another celebration which took place in the fourteenth century when Henry Picard, citizen and Vintner, feasted no less than five Kings. Exact identification of the five Kings has not been firmly established, but the great occasion has never been forgotten. At every Vintners' banquet, therefore, the toast is: 'The Vintners' Company, may it flourish, root and branch, for ever with Five and the Master'. And after the toast it is five cheers (instead of the customary three) that are called for in memory of the Feast of the Five Kings.

The Dyers' Company also hold a Swan Dinner in the autumn which is very similar to the Swan Feast of the Vintners. Instead of a military band playing *Greensleeves*, the musical accompaniment is provided by a baritone rendering of *The Swan*, a song adapted from an early folk tune first published in 1651 in John Playford's *The English Dancing Master*. The words are:

> Look up, my Masters, mark my words
> And hear what we shall sing ye,
> And Liverymen all, both great and small,
> Now mark what they do bring ye.
> A swan, an offering fair they bear
> Avem nobilem nunc cantamus.

The cygnets which provide the ceremonial dish for these Swan Dinners are still grey but fully grown, and their loss comes at a time when the swans' parental enthusiasm has waned. This is the period when the parent swans would drive the cygnets away or kill them if they did not leave, for their dominant wish is, at this point, to preserve their own nesting territory for the next brood.

To return to the more practical aspects of Swan Upping, identification is, of course, by the parent swans. If these have no nicks in the upper beak the cry goes up, 'the Queen's swans', whereupon swans and cygnets are returned to the water and the boats set off in search of the next swan family. To watch the Swan Uppers handling the birds is enlightening, for swans are not gentle birds, especially when they suspect that danger threatens their cygnets. When encountered, the swans and cygnets are usually swimming peacefully in a creek or by an overhung bank of the river – a tranquil little bird family taken entirely by surprise when captured by the skilled Swan Uppers. In a trice swans and cygnets are in the boats, their legs tied, and the adult swans sitting helplessly and silently in the bottom of the boat. Not so the cygnets, for these fluffy grey creatures fear that their last moment has come and they set up a frantic squealing. But they are handled very gently and suffer no pain. The one nick for a Dyers' cygnet or two nicks for a Vintners' bird are carried out swiftly and the pinioning done; then, legs unbound, the swans and cygnets find themselves back in the water. Slightly flustered they gather together, just to ensure that the family is complete, and then they move away as if nothing had happened.

One interesting custom during the Swan Voyage takes place when the boats come within sight of Windsor Castle. At this point all the

Swan Uppers stand to attention in the boats with oars raised, and they salute 'Her Majesty the Queen, Seigneur of the Swans'. Another custom, of a less dignified nature, is that each 'colt' (the term for a 'new boy' on his first Swan Upping) is ducked in the water when he least expects it.

The duties of the three Swan Herdsmen are extensive. John Turk covers the stretch of the river from Windsor to Oxford; Michael Turk from Richmond to Windsor; and Harold Cobb the lower reaches of the Thames. The swans must be looked after at all hours, and duties include rescue of injured or strayed swans; this sometimes means a call from the Police in the middle of the night to collect a swan which has flown and crash-landed on a busy road or railway line. Such tasks come into the category of everyday work; the Swan Upping is work too, but it is also a very fascinating summertime custom of London's river, and one of great antiquity.

Doggett's Coat and Badge Race

River Thames – London Bridge to Chelsea (on or near 1 August)

> *Let your oars like lightning flog it,*
> *Up the Thames as swiftly jog it,*
> *An you'd win the Prize of Doggett,*
> *   The glory of the River.*
> *Bending, bowing, straining, rowing,*
> *Perhaps the wind in fury blowing,*
> *Or the Tide against you flowing,*
> *   The Coat and Badge for ever!*
> (Author unknown)

To see a group of winners of Doggett's Coat and Badge Race, all wearing their distinctive uniform and massive silver badge, is one of the picturesque sights of London. This famous sculling race, which dates from the second decade of the eighteenth century, has been described as the best test on the river of skill in rough water and good steering, for the course is long and there are many bridges to negotiate. It is also claimed to be the oldest race in the world to have been contested without a break. During the war years of this century the race was cancelled, but continuity was achieved by the 1915–1919 races being held consecutively in 1920, and the 1940–1947 races in 1947.

The founder was Thomas Doggett, a popular Irish comedian of the late seventeenth and early eighteenth centuries. It was his affection for the Thames Watermen and enthusiasm for the Hanoverian accession which inspired him to inaugurate the event, to take place each year on the anniversary of George 1's accession to the throne. On 1 August 1715, therefore, the Thames Watermen and their apprentices gathered to read a placard affixed to London Bridge. It stated: 'This being the day of His Majesty's happy accession to the throne there will be given by Mr. Doggett an Orange Colour Livery with a Badge representing Liberty to be rowed for by Six Watermen that are out of their time within the year past. They are to row from London Bridge to Chelsea. It will be continued annually on the same day for ever'.

It is to this race rather than to his acting career that Thomas Doggett owes immortality. He left Dublin as a young man to try his luck on the English stage, and it has sometimes been said that he made his début at Bartholomew Fair; but no record exists of his appearance there until 1702, whereas he was already acting at Drury Lane by 1691. He became joint manager of Drury Lane with Colley Cibber and Robert Wilks – an association as actor-managers which lasted 20 years and was highly successful apart from clashes of temperament between Doggett and Wilks. As an actor he was especially renowned for his skill in make-up. Sir Godfrey Kneller commented that he (Kneller) could only copy nature from the originals before him, while Doggett varied his impersonations at pleasure and yet preserved the likeness. Tony Aston, a member of Doggett's company of strolling players, described him as 'a little, lively spract Man . . . His Behaviour modest, cheerful and complaisant. He sung in Company very agreeably, and in Public very comically . . . He dress'd neat, and something fine – in a plain Cloth Coat and a brocaded Waistcoat . . . He gave his Yearly Water-Badge out of a warm Principle (being a staunch Revolution Whig). I cannot part with this Nonpareil without saying that he was the most faithful, pleasant Actor that ever was . . .' At Fishmongers'

Hall there hangs a portrait in oils of the actor by an unknown artist, but the only authentic likeness is said to be an engraving in George Daniel's *Merrie England* which depicts him dancing the Cheshire Round.

Doggett's Coat and Badge Race owed its origin, so the story goes, to the actor's difficulty, one stormy night, in finding a boat to take him home after the theatre – a Thames journey up-river against the tide. It was a young Waterman who had just completed his apprenticeship (in other words, had just earned his status as a Freeman of the Watermen's Company) who eventually rowed him to Chelsea under these unfavourable conditions, and this incident later inspired Doggett to found a race for first-year Freemen rowed against the tide.

The bond which existed in those days between actors and Watermen was very close, and as the bulk of the theatre audiences travelled by water it is obvious that the players and the men of the river depended a good deal on each other for their prosperity. Without the Watermen the audience would be thin, and when the theatres were closed the trade of the Watermen suffered a slump. It is easily understandable, therefore, that Thomas Doggett's thoughts should have turned to the Watermen when he decided to inaugurate an annual contest in celebration of the Hanoverian accession. By this time he was living in Eltham, Kent, having retired from the stage in about 1714, and in political outlook he had become a staunch Whig. From this Kent retreat he emerged for three professional appearances in March and April 1717; one was in *The Wanton Wife*, performed in the presence of King George I, and the others were return performances in two of his most famous roles, Ben in *Love for Love* and Hob in *The Country Wake*.

On another occasion, when Doggett had come to London from Eltham to watch his Coat and Badge Race, he was molested on his way to the river by the eighteenth-century equivalent of 'muggers'. There is a Pepysian vigour about his own account of the incident: 'As I was making my way through the 'Friars intending to take water at Temple Stairs, in order that I might witness the race for my Coat and Badge, one of those rake helly fellows that so beset the town stopped me, and cocking his hat with arms akimbo cried "Whig or

95

Tory?" He did not care a Queen Anne's farthing for my politics, but made it the pretext for a quarrel. I whipped out my hanger in a trice, set my back to the wall and cried, "Hurray for King George and long life to him", and yet I had liked to have fared scurvily had I not bethought me that my own name for the nonce would stand me in even better stead than the King's. So when, being surrounded by a host of tatterdemalions and pronounced a rat that must bleed, I said be it so, my masters, and though you fail in the recognition, know that I am Doggett, whereat the varlets laughed; true, I escaped with a whole skin, but at the expense of a guinea. This is the gist on't – so now to dinner and afterwards to the White Swan there to drink a cool tankard and shake hands with the winner'.

In September 1721, when Thomas Doggett died, his will provided for the famous race, and the task of administering his bequest fell to the Fishmongers' Company. At the annual November dinner of the Fishmongers, therefore, the winner is ceremonially presented with his Coat and Badge, the scene made all the more memorable by a Guard of Honour of former Doggett winners.

Changes have taken place since the early days of the race. The Coat is now nearer to red than orange. The Badge still displays the word 'Liberty' on a scroll above the White Horse of Hanover, but the original inscription, 'The gift of Thomas Doggett, the late famous comedian, in commemoration of King George's happy accession to the throne of Great Britain' is now omitted. Each Badge is inscribed with the name of the winner, his place of domicile, and the year of his win. Originally competitors could only enter the race once, but a second attempt is now permitted, and entry is no longer restricted to first year Freemen, so that apprentices still serving their time may compete. The race is now rowed *with* the tide instead of against it, and there are numerous bridges to negotiate which did not exist in Doggett's day. The boats are different, too, for in earlier times these were the passenger wherries – heavy and lacking in manoeuvrability compared with the light racing craft used today. They were the boats referred to by Ben Jonson (1573–1637) when he wrote:

> *At Bread Street's Mermaid having dined, and merry,*
> *Proposed to go to Holborn in a wherry.*

Exactly what these wherries looked like can be seen in Peter Monamy's portrait of the first winner of Doggett's Coat and Badge Race which hangs in Watermen's Hall. The name of this first winner is unknown.

One unsatisfactory change in the race was introduced in the eighteenth century and later rectified. In 1769, owing to the large number of entries, it was decided to select the competitors by drawing lots. This often resulted in the finest rowers being eliminated and the Coat and Badge going to a rower of inferior quality. In 1873 trial heats were substituted and today, when these are necessary, they are rowed during the month prior to the race. In the years since the last war another important change has come about – the race has gone over to Amateur status and silver cups now replace the financial prizes originally presented to all competitors who completed the course. But the course remains the same – a distance of four miles five furlongs between the sites of the two Thames-side inns which formerly marked the start and finish, the Old Swan at London Bridge and the White Swan at Chelsea.

Famous names of the river appear in the long list of Doggett winners. For instance, in 1730 the winner was Jack Broughton, who later earned another sporting title, becoming in 1734 Champion Boxer of England. He was known as the father of boxing, and the rules which he established in 1743 became the accepted code for the sport for the next century.

Phelps is a name which crops up again and again among the Doggett winners. In fact, ten members of the Phelps family have been winners since 1860. These were: H. J. M. Phelps (1860); W. Phelps (1875); C. Phelps (1884); Harry Phelps (1919); Tom Phelps (1922); Richard Phelps (1923); Jack Phelps (1928); E. A. (Ted) Phelps (1930); Eric Phelps (1933); Edwin H. Phelps (1938). Ted Phelps also became World Professional Sculling Champion, and Eric Phelps became English Professional Champion. The silver Doggett Badge in the National Maritime Museum at Greenwich is the one which William Phelps won in 1875. His nephew Harry Phelps (winner 1919) was Bargemaster of the Fishmongers' Company from 1927 until his retirement in December 1972 and he was the Starter and Umpire of 46 races. In December 1973 he died suddenly, aged

80, exactly one year after his retirement as Bargemaster – at a function attended by his friends of the river. He was wearing his Doggett Coat and Badge uniform when death came to him; and no member of this famous sculling family could wish for a gentler and more appropriate way to bow out from the river scene.

It was Harry Phelps' brother Tom (Doggett winner, 1922) who will be remembered by the millions who watched Sir Winston Churchill's funeral on television. As the barge carried Sir Winston's body up-river from Tower Pier the solitary figure of Tom Phelps was seen standing alone on the bow, upright and motionless in the bitter wind which prevailed on that sad January day in 1965. As the cranes dipped in salute and the barge moved slowly upstream a commentator remarked that Tom Phelps seemed to be representing all the Watermen of London's river.

The Queen's Bargemaster, H. A. (Bert) Barry (Doggett winner, 1925) was World Professional Sculling Champion from 1928–30 (see p. 66). His brother, Lou Barry (Doggett winner, 1927, and at the time of writing coach to the Cambridge University crew for the past six years) was English Professional Champion. Bert Barry's father, William (Bill) Barry was Doggett winner in 1891, winning the race the hard way, over the tide after high water at London Bridge. In 1896 he was English Professional Champion; in the same year, in Austin, Texas, he won the World Double Scull title and was in the winning crew of the World Four-Oar Championship. Bert Barry's uncle, Ernest Barry (Doggett winner, 1903, and King's Bargemaster) won the World Professional Sculling Championship five times between 1912 and 1920.

With the change to Amateur status new fields opened up for the Doggett winners to conquer, and since that time Charles A. Dearsley (Doggett winner, 1962) and Kenneth Dwan (Doggett winner, 1971) have both won the Amateur Sculling Championship of England; Kenneth Dwan was also Amateur Champion of Great Britain and represented Great Britain at the Olympics in Mexico and Munich.

Doggett's Coat and Badge Race remains one of the great annual events of the river, from the social as well as the sportsman's point of view. Launches gather on the day at the Fishmongers' and Watermen's landing stages at London Bridge and Tower Pier, and these are thronged with the guests of the Fishmongers and the Company of Watermen and Lightermen. It is a grand day for all, and adding colour to the scene are the stalwart figures of many former Doggett's Coat and Badge Winners, wearing with pride the uniform with its great silver badge which is the mark of victory. In a separate launch stands the Fishmongers' Bargemaster, imposingly clad in cocked hat and maroon uniform with blue and gold trimmings, the golden badge of the Fishmongers' Company on his left arm and the Starter's flag in his hand. The signal is given, the boats shoot away – and when the foremost streaks to the winning post at the end of this testing course yet another Waterman will have won the coveted Coat and Badge. This he will have the honour of wearing, on special occasions, for the rest of his life.

Although Thomas Doggett's fame as an actor is now eclipsed, this did not apply for a decade or so after his death, as is evidenced by lines written on a Lambeth windowpane in 1737:

> *Tom Doggett, the greatest sly droll in his parts,*
> *In acting was certain a master of arts;*
> *A monument left – no herald is fuller –*
> *His praise is sung yearly by many a sculler.*
> *Ten thousand years hence if the world last so long*
> *Tom Doggett will still be the theme of their song.*

So Doggett's role as a comedian, and the laughter he evoked, were still as well known 16 years after his death as the race whose fame has since proved so much more enduring.

CHAPTER FOUR

The Services

The Household Division of the Army

No one would deny that the major part of the ceremonial pageantry of London is provided by the Household Division of the Army, the Sovereign's personal Guard – known prior to 1968 as the Household Brigade. It comprises two cavalry regiments and five regiments of foot guards, and from the two cavalry regiments is formed the mounted regiment of the Household Cavalry. The cavalryman's service is divided between periods of mounted and armoured duty at home and abroad, and he handles armoured cars and tanks with the same ease as the shining black horses of his ceremonial role. This separation of ceremonial and active service also applies to the foot guards.

It is the men of the Household Division, in their ceremonial role, who form the Sovereign's Escort and Guard of Honour at the State Opening of Parliament, who parade so superbly during the annual Trooping the Colour ceremony, and whose precision during the Changing of the Guard ceremonies at Buckingham Palace and Whitehall is watched daily by crowds of admiring onlookers.

The two regiments of the Household Cavalry are:

1 *The Life Guards*, who rank first in order of precedence in the British Army and date back to 1659 when formed as the King's Life Guard in exile with the future Charles II. They then consisted of 80 loyalist exiles in Holland whose number, by the time of the Restoration in 1660, had swelled to 600. The Life Guards have a distinguished battle record, one of the most historic episodes in their history being the decisive charge of the Life Guards at the Battle of Waterloo (1815).

2 *The Royal Horse Guards and 1st Dragoons (the Blues and Royals)* were amalgamated into one regiment in 1969.

During the Civil War of the seventeenth century the predecessors of the Royal Horse Guards were the Regiment of Horse on the Cromwellian side. They became part of the King's Army following the Restoration. In 1820 they joined the Life Guards in the Household Cavalry – a distinction accorded to them in honour of their Colonel, the Duke of Wellington, and of their gallantry at the Battle of Waterloo.

The 1st Royal Dragoons were founded in 1661 under the title of 'The Tangier Horse', having been raised for the specific purpose of defending Tangier when it became a Crown possession in the dowry of Charles 11's bride, Catherine of Braganza. In 1684 they returned from Tangier and, under the title of 'His Majesty's Own Royal Regiment of Dragoons', the King gave them precedence over all other cavalry regiments. They have won distinction in many a battle, ranging from the cavalry Charge of the Heavy Brigade at Balaclava in 1854 to trench warfare in the First World War and mechanised action in the Western Desert and North West Europe in the Second World War.

To anyone uninitiated in Army lore the description 'Blues and Royals' is somewhat confusing – the Royal Horse Guards being 'the Blues' whereas the Dragoons are 'the Royals'. Whether Life Guards, Blues or Royals, they are all superb cavalrymen, and to come upon a detachment of the Household Cavalry – riding along the Mall to Horse Guards with a marvellous clattering of hoofs and waving of plumes – is one of the grand sights of London.

The five regiments of the Guards Division (foot guards) are composed of:

1 *The Grenadier Guards*, raised by the future Charles 11 in 1656 from loyalists who followed him to Bruges. They took the title of the Royal Regiment of Guards. Their history, with its record of 76 Battle Honours, dates back earlier, therefore, than the mounted Life Guards, who were also founded by Charles 11 in exile. At the Battle of Waterloo the regiment defeated the

Grenadiers of Napoleon's Imperial Guard, and their present title was officially assumed after this victory.

2 *The Coldstream Guards* have a record of continuous service since 1650 when they were raised as Monck's Regiment of Foot in Cromwell's New Model Army. In January 1660 (year of the Restoration of the Monarchy) they were quartered at Coldstream, the Scottish border town which eventually supplied the name of the regiment. Led by General Monck they marched south to London, and under his leadership set about restoring order in the capital. On 23 May General Monck was on the beach at Dover to welcome Charles ii back to England, and he was thereafter created Duke of Albemarle and Captain General of the Land Forces. In due course Cromwell's New Model Army was disbanded but Monck's Regiment of Foot was maintained until 1661, when the men paraded before the King on Tower Hill and laid down their arms. They were ordered to take them up again as the Lord General's Regiment of Foot Guards and the Lord General's Troop of Horse Guards (the latter eventually being merged into the Life Guards). They remained under Monck's leadership until his death in 1670. Since then their title has remained the Coldstream Guards.

3 *The Scots Guards* were founded earliest of all – in 1642 by Charles i. After the King's execution they remained loyal to the Royalist cause, fighting at Dunbar and Worcester, then dispersing during the period of the Cromwellian régime, and emerging again on the Restoration as the Scottish Regiment of Foot Guards. The regiment bore various titles until, in 1877, they finally became the Scots Guards. They have won 90 Battle Honours, 39 of which are recorded on their Colours.

4 *The Irish Guards* were formed by Queen Victoria at the turn of the century in recognition of the valour of the Irish troops who served in the campaigns of the Boer War. In the two World Wars of this century the regiment won six Victoria Crosses. Their Irish wolfhound is the only parade mascot in the Household Division.

5 *The Welsh Guards* came into being in 1915, on the express

wish of King George v that the Principality should have its own regiment. Welshmen had been stalwart fighters in other regiments prior to this, and after their formation as the Welsh Guards their first Victoria Cross was won at Pilckem (1917). In the Second World War the Welsh Guards made what has been described as a record armoured advance; in one day they covered 100 miles and were the first British troops to enter Brussels on 3 September 1944.

A number of customs have developed through the years in the different regiments. A Grenadier, for instance, when answering a question never uses the words 'Yes' or 'No' but always says 'Sir'; his meaning must be judged by the intonation of his voice. A Coldstreamer, on the other hand, makes a point of saying 'Yes, Sir' and 'No, Sir'. The plural of Grenadier is Grenadiers, whereas Coldstream Guards are never Coldstreams, but are always Coldstreamers.

The Blues and Royals are unique in being the only regiment who salute their Officers when not wearing hats. This stems from one of their famous charges when the Commanding Officer lost his hat during the charge; when reporting to the Army Commander that the attack had been successful, he rode up bareheaded and saluted him. And so the custom has survived.

The seven regiments of the Household Division, cavalry and foot, each have their own very accomplished and renowned regimental band, and these include the pipers of the Scots and Irish Guards. The Pipe Major of the Scots Guards holds the title of Household Piper to Her Majesty The Queen, and in this role he is piper at State Banquets. The Welsh Guards, true to the choral tradition of Wales, have a Battalion Choir. But most spectacular of all, visibly, are the mounted bands of the two cavalry regiments. These are led by the great Drum Horses (always skewbald or piebald) which bear the solid silver kettle drums presented by two monarchs, George III and William IV. Bringing up the rear of the cavalry column on ceremonial occasions is a figure as striking as the Drum Major on his Drum Horse; this is the Farrier, who bears in his hand a pole-axe, its blade gleaming in the sunshine.

Londoners and visitors to London tend to visualise the Household

Division only in its ceremonial role, but it should be remembered that these regiments are also stationed in many parts of the world on active service, and the history of each regiment speaks for itself.

Trooping the Colour

Greatest day of the year for watching the pageantry of the Household Division is the Trooping the Colour Ceremony which celebrates the Sovereign's official birthday. This takes place each year on a Saturday morning in June (the Queen's actual birthday is in April), and the best viewpoint is, of course, a reserved seat on Horse Guards Parade, where the ceremony takes place. Tickets are scarce, but there is unreserved space and standing room for those who arrive early, and only from the Horse Guards vantage point can be appreciated to the full this magnificent parade and the remarkable precision of the Guards as they march and countermarch to the music of the massed bands. The ceremony is too long and intricate to describe here in detail, but it opens when Her Majesty arrives on the parade ground at 11 am, attended by the Sovereign's Escort of the Household Cavalry. As the Queen reaches the Saluting Base the bands play the National Anthem and a Royal Salute is fired. She then inspects the parade and on returning to the Saluting Base the whole matchless spectacle of the Birthday Parade unfolds. As it draws to a close each regiment passes before the Queen at the Saluting Base – the foot guards in slow and quick time, the cavalry regiments progressing from a slow pace to a trot.

No reserved seats – or, in fact, any tickets at all – are needed for the almost equally grand yet more intimate spectacle of the procession as it passes along the Mall from Buckingham Palace to Horse Guards. It is not even necessary to arrive especially early, for the lure of the television screen keeps many at home. But the stalwart enthusiasts who line the Mall year after year for the Queen's Birthday Parade gain a marvellous view of the Queen as she rides side-saddle along the centre of this great processional route, and there is also a thrilling close view of the regiments as they pass. The Mall is by far the most exciting place for children to watch the Trooping procession, and the good-natured Mall 'regulars' can usually be relied upon

12   *Remembrance Sunday – The Queen at the Cenotaph Memorial Service for the men of all three Services and the Allied Nations who died in the two World Wars.*

to give them a place on the front of the pavement. The Duke of Edinburgh rides second only to the Queen, and other members of the royal family precede the Queen to and from Horse Guards in open carriages or closed cars. Especially stirring is the moment when the mounted bands ride by, the Drum Horses at the head and the riders handling both horse and instrument with equal ease.

There is a second chance to see the Trooping the Colour procession when it returns to Buckingham Palace, and for the crowds who congregate before the Palace there is also the opportunity to watch the Queen taking the salute at the gates. Later comes the moment, always eagerly awaited by expectant crowds, when the Queen, the Duke of Edinburgh, the Queen Mother, and other members of the royal family appear on the balcony.

Although all seven regiments of the Household Division take part in the Trooping the Colour ceremony it is only one Colour of the foot guards that is trooped, and the turn comes round in rotation. The Queen, as Colonel-in-Chief of each regiment, always wears the uniform of the one whose Colour is being trooped.

It was in 1805 that the Trooping the Colour ceremony first took its present form as a celebration of the Sovereign's official birthday. The origin of the parade goes back to much earlier times, for it once had a very practical purpose – the display of the regimental flag to the fighting men in order that they would be familiar with it as a rallying point on the field of battle. The last time that the Colours were carried into action was during the Crimean War of the 1850s. Since that time the Colour has become a symbol of the pride and tradition of each regiment, and it bears the record of Battle Honours. The Colour is, in fact, the most treasured emblem of the regiment.

Each regiment of foot has a Queen's Colour in addition to its Regimental Colour, and this is carried by the Queen's Guard when the Court is in residence and on royal anniversaries; when the Regimental Colour is carried it is an indication that the Court is not in residence. The three senior regiments of foot guards – the Grenadiers, Coldstream and Scots Guards – also have State Colours which are used only in the presence of the Queen. The Household Cavalry has a Standard for each squadron, and in addition the two regiments each have their own Sovereign's Standard.

13   (*above*) *Trafalgar Night Dinner at the Royal Naval College, Greenwich.*
14   (*below*) *Founder's Day, Royal Hospital, Chelsea.*

The Changing of the Guard

This ceremony is so immensely popular with visitors to London that one aspect should be made clear – it is usually carried out by the Sovereign's personal Guard and is on a reduced scale when the Queen is not in residence. It is important, therefore, to keep an eye on the newspapers and to attend the Changing of the Guard when the Queen is in London. The final clue is, of course, whether or not the Royal Standard is flying from the roof of Buckingham Palace.

It is the foot guards who undertake guard duties at Buckingham Palace, St James's Palace, and the Tower of London and the main viewpoint is, needless to say, Buckingham Palace. Two detachments mount the Queen's Guard in the Forecourt of Buckingham Palace – the St James's Palace Detachment and the Buckingham Palace Detachment. The former is the senior, for St James's Palace was the official residence of the Sovereign from 1698 until Queen Victoria made Buckingham Palace the London residence of the Royal Family, and the Court remains the Court of St James's. Here, therefore, is the headquarters of the Captain of the Queen's Guard, and here the Colour is lodged.

At 11 am the St James's Palace Detachment of the Old Guard forms in Ambassador's Court, St James's, and then, bearing the Colour, marches along the Mall led by the Corps of Drums. At the same time the Buckingham Palace Detachment of the Old Guard has assembled for inspection in the Forecourt of the Palace. Both Detachments then await the arrival of the New Guard in the Forecourt of Buckingham Palace.

The New Guard, with its Regimental Band and Corps of Drums, arrives at 11.30 am and advances in slow-time towards the Old Guard, while the band plays the traditional slow march of the regiment mounting guard. Then follows the symbolic handing over of the Palace keys, posting of sentries, special orders are read, and throughout the Regimental Band keeps the whole ceremony attractively alive. The Old Guard then returns to barracks led by the Regimental Band and Corps of Drums, and the St James's Palace

Detachment of the New Guard marches to St James's Palace, where the Colour is once more lodged in the Guard Room.

There are one or two features to look out for during the Changing of the Guard. For instance, if the regiment concerned is commemorating the anniversary of one of its victories on the field of battle a wreath will ornament the top of the Colour. And if it should be the Irish Guards who are on guard duty, then their Irish wolfhound mascot will be seen marching at the head of the regimental band. Each regiment can be identified by its badge and by the colour of the plume on the bearskin: the Grenadiers, white plume (on left side of bearskin); Coldstream Guards, red plume (on right of bearskin); Scots Guards, no plume; Irish Guards, blue plume (right-hand side); Welsh Guards, green and white plume (left-hand side). A sharp-eyed onlooker can also identify the men by their tunic buttons. The Grenadiers have eight evenly spaced tunic buttons; the Coldstream Guards' buttons are grouped in pairs; the Scots Guards' buttons are in groups of three; the Irish Guards have eight buttons, in two groups of four; and the Welsh Guards have ten buttons in groups of five.

The Life Guards and the Blues and Royals mount guard at Horse Guards, Whitehall, and the scale of the Changing ceremony depends, as at Buckingham Palace, on the Queen being in London. The Changing of the Long Guard is the ceremony to see, for when the Queen is away from London a smaller guard, known as a Short Guard, is on duty and the ceremony is on a lesser scale.

The Changing of the Guard at Whitehall takes place at 11 am on weekdays and 10 am on Sundays, and the location is the yard between the sentry boxes and the clock tower. The Life Guards and the Blues and Royals undertake alternate guard duty and for the Changing of the Guard ceremony the horses of the Old and New Guards line up in two lines facing each other; the Standards are saluted, the mounted sentries are posted, and the Old Guard then sets off along the Mall back to barracks.

In winter the Household Cavalry are not so colourful in appearance as in summer, the riders being shrouded in their long winter cloaks. Nevertheless, cloaked or not, they are a grand sight to encounter on a crisp winter morning. The foot guards also present a more sombre picture in winter, their dark winter coats covering the bright scarlet tunics.

Beating Retreat

Second only to Trooping the Colour as a parade of Service pageantry and precision is the ceremony of Beating Retreat. This is performed on Horse Guards Parade each year by the Household Division and it provides a grand display, made all the more stirring by the music of mounted bands, trumpeters, massed bands, and pipes and drums. The parade usually takes place in late May or early June, and then, about a couple of weeks later, it is customary for another regiment or arm of the Services to Beat Retreat. Every third year, in June, the ceremony is performed by the Royal Marines in honour of the birthday of their Captain General, The Prince Philip, Duke of Edinburgh, who attends in person and takes the salute.

The title of the ceremony has nothing to do with defeat or retreat from the field of battle. It is the retreat of daylight and the onset of night that is signalled or 'beaten', as was the custom in times long past. The ceremony developed and gained its title from the Drummers' signal for the disengagement of forces at nightfall and the posting of the night sentries – an operation which, in the sixteenth-century *Rules and Ordynances for the Warre*, was referred to as 'Watch Setting' rather than Beating Retreat. Not only on the field of battle but in any town, port, castle or fortress that was garrisoned, this was the signal of night. An order of 1727 states that '. . . half an hour before the setting of the sun the Drummers and Port-Guards are to go upon the ramparts and beat a Retreat to give notice to those without that the gates are to be shut'. The purpose of Beating Retreat was then entirely practical; the present-day Horse Guards Parade ceremony is a military display and much grander in scale, but the motive is the same. When the Evening Hymn and Last Post sound over this great parade ground and the Corps of Drums beats during dispersal, we know, as did the armed forces of earlier times, that the day is over and darkness is about to fall.

Royal Salutes

London's Royal Salutes are fired in Hyde Park by the King's Troop, Royal Horse Artillery, and at the Tower of London by the Honourable Artillery Company.

There is an interesting story behind the title of the King's Troop, Royal Horse Artillery – who remained the King's Troop after the accession of Queen Elizabeth II. They were originally known as the Riding Troop, Royal Horse Artillery. The Riding Troop was disbanded on the outbreak of war in 1939, and its revival after the war was due to King George VI's special affection for the Royal Horse Artillery and his wish that an RHA Battery mounted and equipped in the old style should once more fire Royal Salutes in Hyde Park on State occasions.

The first few post-war Royal Salutes were fired under the original title of the Riding Troop, and it was on 24 October 1947 that the name changed. On that day the King honoured the Troop by visiting St John's Wood Barracks. He stayed to Luncheon in the Officers' Mess, and when signing the Visitors' Book he hesitated for a moment as he studied the name of the Riding Troop inscribed in it – then he struck out the word 'Riding' and in its place inserted 'King's'. The King's Troop it has remained, for on the death of King George VI and the accession of Queen Elizabeth II, the Queen expressed the wish that during her lifetime the title should remain unchanged – in memory of her father and as a mark of his particular affection for the RHA and the Troop. There is, therefore, a unique quality about the King's Troop of the RHA. It was raised after the last war on a Sovereign's special request, and it was named personally by that Sovereign, the title being confirmed by his successor.

A Royal Salute fired by the King's Troop in Hyde Park is an exciting event to watch. Six guns and limbers are driven to the Park and for the Salute up to 70 horses and men take part in the operation. It is a grand sight to see the line of horses galloping across the Park to the Saluting Station when the Salute is about to be fired.

The number of rounds fired for a Royal Salute varies according to location. The King's Troop fire a 41 gun Salute in Hyde Park, 21 guns as a Royal Salute and 20 for the capital. When they fire a Royal Salute in the Home Park at Windsor, on the other hand, this is a normal 21 gun Royal Salute. The Honourable Artillery Company fire a Royal Salute of 62 rounds at the Tower of London – 41 rounds in view of the fact that the Tower is a royal residence, and another 21 rounds for the City of London, making a 62 gun Salute in all. (At Windsor the section of the Home Park where the salute is fired is not a royal park – hence the 21 gun Salute.) The King's Troop fire in Hyde Park at 12 o'clock and the HAC at the Tower at 1 pm.

The occasions for the Royal Salutes are the anniversaries of birth of the Queen, the Duke of Edinburgh, Queen Elizabeth the Queen Mother, anniversaries of the Queen's accession to the throne and of her coronation; also for the State Opening of Parliament and State Visits. Guns of the King's Troop, RHA, also fire from Horse Guards Parade to mark the Two Minutes Silence on Remembrance Sunday. For Her Majesty's Birthday Parade in June the Troop fire a Salute in Hyde Park while the foot guards Troop the Colour on Horse Guards Parade.

The Cenotaph Ceremony – Remembrance Sunday

Whitehall – on or near 11 November

This is one of the most moving ceremonies of the year – the memorial service for the men of all three Services and of the Allied Nations who died in the two World Wars of this century. There are present for this ceremony, beside the Cenotaph memorial in Whitehall, detachments of the Royal Navy, Royal Marines, the Army, the Territorial and Army Volunteer Reserve, the Royal Air Force and Royal Auxiliary Air Force, the Royal Observer Corps, the Merchant Navy and Fishing Fleets, the Merchant Air Service, and detachments of ex-Servicemen and women. The Queen, unless unavoidably absent from London, is always present to lay her wreath beside the Cenotaph on Remembrance Sunday.

People begin to gather in Whitehall quite early on this day.

Massed Bands of the Guards Division play to the assembled crowds, and at 10.59 am the Queen reaches the Cenotaph. At 11 am a gun, fired by the King's Troop of the Royal Horse Artillery from Horse Guards Parade, indicates the beginning of the Two Minutes Silence, and at its end, at 11.02 am, a second gun is fired, and the Buglers of the Royal Marines sound the Last Post. Then, with simple dignity, the Queen steps forward to place a wreath by the Cenotaph, followed by members of the Royal Family or their representatives. And afterwards wreaths are laid on behalf of the Governments of the United Kingdom and the Commonwealth, the Royal Navy, the Army, the Royal Air Force, the Merchant Navy and Fishing Fleets, the Merchant Air Services and the Civilian Services – all to the sombre music of a funeral march played by the Massed Bands of the Guards Division. Other wreaths are laid when the Queen has retired.

The Crowds who throng almost every inch of Whitehall on this Remembrance Sunday are, most of them, deep in memories of the men they lost. It is an intensely moving occasion, and there is nothing to match actually being in Whitehall on this day, even if the dense crowds make it impossible to approach anywhere near the Cenotaph. The service is relayed on loud speakers, which means that, even if the wreath-laying ceremony is invisible, everyone is able to take part; and the great crowds of people gathered in Whitehall sing the hymns and have a great sense of participation. The moment when the Minute Gun is fired, and silence falls – broken only by the flight and song of a bird, or the voice of a child too young to understand the significance of the sudden silence – is moving in a way that can only be understood by those who attend the Cenotaph ceremony in person.

Trafalgar Day *(21 October)*

As an island race the British have always owed much of their freedom to naval defence. For this reason the Royal Navy is not only the Senior Service and the oldest of the three services, but it holds a special place in the hearts of the people. Never was that sense of pride and gratitude more overwhelming than when the news spread throughout the kingdom of Admiral Lord Nelson's great victory at the Battle of Trafalgar on 21 October 1805. Napoleon's invasion forces, which had gathered so menacingly on the French side of the Channel, became no longer an imminent threat, and Nelson, killed in the hour of victory, was the hero of every home in the land. Later his body was brought to Greenwich, to the gracious Thames-side building which is now the Royal Naval College but was, from 1705 to 1873, the Greenwich Hospital for aged and disabled seamen. Here, in the dignified setting of the Painted Hall, his body lay in state before being conveyed from Greenwich to Whitehall in all the grave dignity of a massive river procession. That night, eve of the state funeral, Nelson's body lay in the Admiralty, in what is now known as the Nelson Room. The next day, amidst pomp and universal mourning, the hero of Trafalgar was brought to his last resting place in the crypt of St Paul's Cathedral.

In the years that have passed since that date ships and establishments of the Royal Navy celebrate Trafalgar Day and 'The Immortal Memory' each October. There have been other great naval battles and other great victories, but this normally remains the most important naval anniversary of all.

At the Royal Naval College at Greenwich, so closely associated with the days of mourning for Nelson, there is an annual Commemoration Service and a Trafalgar Night Dinner. The latter (which takes place on the Thursday evening nearest to 21 October) is held in the Painted Hall where Nelson lay in state; but this is a cheerful occasion, celebrating the Trafalgar victory rather than mourning the death of Nelson. A distinguished speaker attends, usually a high ranking Naval Officer, and it is he who proposes the toast to 'The Immortal Memory'. Part of the tradition of this Trafalgar Night Dinner at Greenwich is the unfailing presence of a baron of beef, borne by the Chefs and escorted by Sea Cadets clad in the seaman's uniform of Nelson's time. Led by Drummers of the Royal Marines, this little procession slow marches round the Hall to the tune of *The Roast Beef of Old England*, played by a Royal Marines Band.

At the end of the Dinner, when the tables have been cleared, decanters of Port are brought in and this is the time for the toasts.

The Loyal Toast is in two parts. The President of the Dinner addresses the Vice President (seated at the remote end of the Painted Hall) with the words, 'Mr Vice – The Queen'. The band plays the National Anthem, and then the Vice President completes the Toast with 'Ladies and Gentlemen – The Queen'. This Loyal Toast procedure, in which the President addresses the Vice President, and the Vice President then addresses the rest of the diners, is a custom which prevails in most Service messes. Unique in the Services, however, is the Navy custom of remaining seated during the Loyal Toast and throughout the National Anthem – a procedure guaranteed to mystify anyone not versed in naval observances. This originated in the days when the deckheads of ships were so low that no one could stand upright without danger of a cracked head. A dispensation was therefore granted, and the custom has survived into the era of higher deckheads. (This Loyal Toast custom of remaining seated is also observed in two of the Inns of Court, see p. 148.)

The Trafalgar Day Commemoration Service at Greenwich takes place in the Chapel of the Royal Naval College on the Sunday nearest to 21 October. Nelson's Prayer before the Battle of Trafalgar is always included, and his words were: 'May the Great God whom I worship grant to my country, and for the benefit of Europe in general, a great and glorious victory; and may no misconduct in anyone tarnish it; and may humanity after victory be the predominant feature in the British Fleet. For myself, individually, I commit my life to Him that made me, and may His blessing alight on my endeavours for serving my country faithfully. To Him I resign myself and the just cause which he entrusted to me to defend'.

HMS *President*, berthed near Blackfriars Bridge, is headquarters of the London Division of the Royal Naval Reserve, and each year a Trafalgar Night Dinner is held on board, to which distinguished guests are invited.

In Trafalgar Square, where Landseer's lions guard the base of Nelson's Column, an annual Trafalgar Sunday Commemoration Service and wreath-laying ceremony is held. This is a Navy League ceremony, and usually taking part are several hundred Sea Cadets and about 80 or so members of the Girls Nautical Training Corps. A Royal Marines Band provides the music, and the ceremony is attended by either the First Sea Lord or the Second Sea Lord (in alternate years), together with the Chairman of the Navy League, Naval dignitaries, Commonwealth High Commissioners and other representatives. The Lord Mayor of the City of Westminster usually attends. By 11.20 am they have all gathered beneath Nelson's Column, and the procession, which assembles on Horse Guards Parade, has reached the Square.

The service commences with a fanfare by the Buglers of the Royal Marines, followed by an address (by the First Sea Lord or the Second Sea Lord, according to the year of attendance), the Last Post, the wreath-laying and the hymn for those in peril on the sea, in which the public gathered around the balustrades of Trafalgar Square are invited to join. Then follows Nelson's Prayer and finally the National Anthem.

Throughout the whole ceremony the flourishing community of Trafalgar Square pigeons cluster wherever they can find space, obviously ill-used at being displaced from their home ground; and at every sudden burst of music from the Royal Marines Band they rise into the sky, in a cloud of flapping wings, to wheel around Lord Nelson's head as he stands on his aloof and lofty height. Unfortunately he *does* seem aloof, for he faces Whitehall and Westminster, with his back turned resolutely to the ceremony. Nevertheless, he seems to be casting an approving eye along Whitehall as the youthful procession, with its potential sailors of the Navy of the future, comes marching to the Square to honour him and his victory. This part of London is true naval territory, for Nelson's statue faces the Old Admiralty building where his body lay on the night prior to the state funeral. The Admiralty Arch provides a grand entrance to the Mall, and all along this processional route, between Trafalgar Square and Buckingham Palace, metal ship models surmount the lamp standards. Just inside the Admiralty Arch is the statue of another great sailor, Captain James Cook, first circumnavigator of the world.

Closely linked with Trafalgar Day is the National Service for Seafarers, which takes place each year on the Wednesday nearest to 21 October. It is always held in St Paul's Cathedral, burial place of Lord Nelson, and is a service for all whose life is spent at sea – the men of the Navy, the Merchant Service, the Fishing Fleet, the Pilots and Lighthouse Keepers, the men of the Lifeboats. This Service was inaugurated in 1905 (centenary of the Battle of Trafalgar) and has continued annually ever since, except during the years of the two World Wars (when broadcast services took its place). The Lord Mayor attends, the sermon is always preached by a Bishop, and nautical parties from the various Nautical Schools throughout the country carry their Colours, forming up outside the entrance to the Cathedral and walking in procession to the High Altar, where the Colours are received. The Choir is provided by Naval Schools. Included in the Service is a Prayer for Seafarers and the Prayer used daily in Her Majesty's Navy, and finally, during the singing of the seafarers' hymn, the Colours are returned to the bearers and then the National Anthem is sung. Before and after the Service a Royal Marines Band plays in the North Transept.

The Royal Navy is not seen in ceremonial mood in London as frequently as the Army, but when the Royal Marines Beat Retreat on Horse Guards Parade this is a grand opportunity to see them at their ceremonial best. On all occasions when there are great State processions – and especially, of course, on the Coronation of the Sovereign – the Royal Navy and the Royal Marines participate; and on the sadder occasion of the death of the Sovereign (also, as a special case in recent times, on the death of Sir Winston Churchill) a Royal Navy contingent has the honour of drawing the gun carriage which bears the coffin.

The Royal Air Force and Battle of Britain Sunday

(A Sunday in mid-September)
The Royal Air Force is the youngest of the Services and cannot be expected to have any old customs, but the commemoration of Battle of Britain Sunday will certainly become one in the years ahead, for this heroic campaign of 'the few' will always be remembered among the great victories of warfare. To those who remember personally, those autumn days of 1940 stand out indelibly in the memory. I can still visualise, as if it were yesterday, the scene as I stood in a garden

and gazed up at the blue September sky where part of this historic battle was being fought out. All over Britain there are commemorative services on this Battle of Britain Sunday, and in London the most important are at Westminster Abbey and at the RAF's own church, St Clement Danes in the Strand.

The RAF, as I have already said, is very youthful compared with the Navy and the Army, and there is no better way of following its development than to visit the RAF Museum at Hendon, opened by Her Majesty The Queen on 15 November 1972. Here are aircraft of earliest to latest types, and one of the original hangars of Graham White's School of Flying at Hendon has been preserved and forms part of the Museum – representing one of the oldest aircraft hangars in the world in continuous use. Britain's Air Force began on 1 April 1911 when the Air Battalion of the Royal Engineers was formed, with headquarters and No 1 Airship Company at Farnborough, Hampshire, and No 2 Aeroplane Company at Larkhill, on Salisbury Plain, Wiltshire. A month before this, Naval flying instruction had started at Eastchurch in the Isle of Sheppey, and the Naval Flying School was opened at Eastchurch during the following December. The formation of the Royal Flying Corps, comprising a Military and Naval Wing, a Reserve, and the Royal Aircraft Factory at Farnborough, was authorised by Royal Warrant on 13 April 1912. On 1 April 1918 the Royal Air Force was founded by amalgamation of the Royal Flying Corps and the Royal Naval Air Service.

As far as London ceremonial is concerned, on State occasions the RAF contributes its share of route-lining duties with the other Services, and on State Visits to this country the Guard of Honour at the airport is provided by the Queen's Colour Squadron, a ceremonial unit of the Royal Air Force Regiment. For the Lord Mayor's Show a 48-strong contingent of RAF apprentices (training in such aspects as engineering) usually marches in the procession, and two RAF Bands are provided, one marching and the other stationed near the Church of St Clement Danes. But the most dramatic impact of the RAF on the London ceremonial scene is on the June occasion of the Queen's Birthday Parade (the Trooping the Colour ceremony). Usually exactly at 1 o'clock aircraft of the Royal Air Force Strike Command salute Her Majesty The Queen in a fly-past over the centre of London and over Buckingham Palace, more or less on a line with the Mall.

St Clement Danes is the central church of the RAF. This beautiful Wren church was burnt out by fire bombs during one of the air raids of 1941 and, after sufficient funds had been raised for rebuilding and restoration around the shell that was left, it was reconsecrated in 1958. The floor is inlaid with nearly 800 squadron and unit badges carved in Welsh slate, and a rosette of Commonwealth Air Force badges surrounds that of the RAF at the West Door. In St Clement Danes are recorded the names of the fallen and of those who were awarded the Victoria Cross and George Cross.

The Honourable Artillery Company

This famous Army volunteer unit must figure in any description of London's ceremonies and customs, for it is the HAC's Company of Pikemen and Musketeers who add so picturesquely to the scene on occasions of state ceremonial in the City, and the HAC Gunners who fire the Royal Salutes at the Tower of London. The HAC is a 'privileged Regiment' in the City of London, which means that it shares the right with only five other Regiments in the British Army and the Royal Marines to march through the City with drums beating, bayonets fixed and colours flying.

The Honourable Artillery Company is the oldest fighting unit in the Kingdom – the senior volunteer unit and certainly the most renowned. When the Company received its Charter from Henry VIII in 1537 its title was the Fraternity or Guild of Longbows, Crossbows and Handguns. There was motive in the timing of the King's Charter, for his rift with the Pope had caused religious dissension throughout the realm, and he was anxious to keep the trained bands of London on his side. In due course the name became the Gentlemen of the Artillery Garden, and then merely the Artillery Company. The 'Honourable' part of the title did not receive royal confirmation until the reign of Queen Victoria, but it had been in use since 1685.

The HAC's history dates back even earlier than Henry VIII's Charter, for prior to 1537 the Company existed as a body of citizen archers known as the Guild of St George. They played their part in many a battle, and it is said that they gave valiant service at the Battle of Crécy. These citizen soldiers of pre-Tudor date can be regarded as the ancestors of the Territorial Army of today.

The Artillery Garden which formed part of the Company's early title was located on land where Spitalfields Market now stands – an open training ground shared with the Yeomen of the Guard of the Tower. This was not a satisfactory arrangement, and in the seventeenth century the Artillery Company petitioned the Lord Mayor and City Corporation for land of their own. They were allocated the third field in Moorfields, of which they took possession at the end of the Civil War; and here Armoury House, headquarters of the HAC, was built in 1735. It was a rare privilege, then as now, for a military unit to possess its own property, and the HAC's association with the City Corporation has remained very close, the Lord Mayor and Sheriffs always being *ex officio* members of the Court of Assistants by which the HAC is governed.

There has also been a tradition of close royal association since the seventeenth century. It was in 1641 that Charles I (well aware of the Parliamentary loyalties of the City) enrolled as members of the Artillery Company his two sons, Charles Prince of Wales and James Duke of York (aged eleven and seven respectively). As in the case of Henry VIII's Charter it is clear that the King hoped to win a Royalist following in the City. This proved in vain. The City sided with Parliament during the Civil War, and its Train Bands, officered by the Artillery Company, won special distinction at the Battle of Newbury, where they held their ground and beat back the charges of Prince Rupert's cavalry.

On the Restoration of the Monarchy in 1660 the Duke of York (later James II) became Captain General of the Company. Prince Rupert, doubtless remembering with respect the resistance offered to his cavalry at Newbury, also became a member. Since then the office of Captain General has always been filled by the Sovereign or a near relative, and the Queen, who fulfils this role so graciously today, is the first female Captain General in the records of the Company. The Prince of Wales joined the HAC in 1970, but he had already come to Armoury House when 11 years old, following the precedent set in 1641 by the former Charles, Prince of Wales.

The only person ever to be made an Honorary Member of the HAC was Lunardi, the balloonist, who on 15 September 1784 made his historic balloon ascent from the HAC grounds. A contemporary colour engraving hangs in Armoury House which shows Lunardi and his balloon rising triumphantly from the ground; Armoury House is seen in the background, and the astonished onlookers gaze upwards at 'the first traveller in the English atmosphere'.

Another picture in Armoury House depicts the scene on the HAC's training ground when, in 1780, the City Corporation expressed gratitude for the Company's aid in quelling the Gordon Riots by presenting two brass field pieces (cannon). These were the first pieces of artillery, in the modern sense of the word, that the Company ever possessed. They now occupy a place of honour on the Great Staircase at Armoury House.

Also a treasured relic, preserved at the top of these stairs, is the ship's bell of SS *Westmeath*, the vessel in which the 1st Battalion of the HAC sailed for France on 18 September 1914. Survivors continue to meet at Armoury House each 18 September. They are becoming reduced in numbers but still produce a good muster – and they intend to go on meeting until only two are left. Yet another relic is a curious stone object which is the last surviving 'Rover' stone – a medieval archery mark once used for target practice. Each was named, and this last survivor is entitled 'Scarlet'.

Today the HAC comprises three Royal Horse Artillery Batteries, three Infantry Companies, an Officer Training Wing, an Officer Pool, the HAC detachment of the Metropolitan Special Constabulary, and the Company of Pikemen and Musketeers. In earlier times the bowmen and pikemen were among the stoutest fighters of the Company, and in 1925 it was decided to form this ceremonial unit, in order to revive the traditions of these members of the Artillery Company of centuries ago. The Company of Pikemen and Musketeers is composed of men of the Veteran Company of the HAC and the uniform and drill is identical to that of the pikemen of the sixteenth and seventeenth centuries. Shortly after the Coronation of

1953 the Queen recognised the Company of Pikemen and Musketeers by Royal Warrant, establishing their role as 'part of the military parade on great occasions of state and on other ceremonial occasions'. They are a grand sight, with their pikes and glinting armour, and the Lord Mayor would not look half so splendid in his gold coach on Lord Mayor's Day without the Pikemen as escort. They form a Guard of Honour inside Guildhall or the Mansion House during State Visits to the City by members of the Royal Family or Heads of Foreign States. The Active Unit of the HAC provides the Guard of Honour outside the building on these occasions.

In the Long Room at Armoury House hang portraits of past Captain Generals together with the Colours of the Company – among them the Stars and Stripes of the USA. In 1628 Robert Keayne, a member of the Artillery Company, emigrated to the New World, and 10 years later he founded, in Boston, The Ancient and Honourable Artillery Company of Massachusetts, daughter Company of the HAC. Its Charter was granted by Governor Winthrop, and Robert Keayne was appointed the first Captain General.

Every member of the HAC, royalty or commoner, signs his name for posterity on vellum, a custom started in 1635. The old Vellum Book of 1660–88 reveals a remarkable list of notabilities of the Restoration period, and the HAC has, in fact, always preserved a unique quality of distinction. Anyone who doubts it has only to look at the Vellum Book.

The Royal Hospital, Chelsea – Founder's Day and other customs

(Founder's Day, on or near 29 May)

The very existence of the Royal Hospital, Chelsea, is an old custom, as are the familiar red-coated uniforms of the Chelsea Pensioners and the celebrations on Founder's Day. This occasion, also known as Oak Apple Day, takes place each year on 29 May, or as near as possible to that date, for this is not only the anniversary of King Charles II's birthday but also of his restoration to the throne in 1660. The oak leaf sprigs which every Pensioner wears on Founder's

15 *The Judges' Procession at Westminster, which marks the opening of the new legal year.*

16 *Quit Rents. The City Solicitor splits hazel twigs with a hatchet and later counts six horseshoes and 61 nails in the annual rendering of two ancient Quit Rents at the Royal Courts of Justice.*

Day are symbolic of the oak tree at Boscobel House, Shropshire, which concealed him from the eyes of the Cromwellian soldiers after the Battle of Worcester (1651).

The Founder's Day Parade of the old soldiers has been carried out without a break since 1692, even through the two World Wars of this century. On this day the statue of King Charles II by Grinling Gibbons in Figure Court is almost concealed beneath its ceremonial dress of oak leaves; and at dinner on Founder's Day every Pensioner, by tradition, is served with plum pudding and an extra pint of beer.

The Pensioners parade in Figure Court at 10.50 am under the command of the Adjutant. They form four Companies under their respective Captain of Invalids, and those unable to march owing to age or disability occupy the seats which frame the Parade Ground. When the Parade and speeches are over the Pensioners all remove head-dress and give three hearty cheers for 'Our pious Founder, King Charles II', and then for Her Majesty the Queen. A member of the Royal Family or a high-ranking Army Officer takes the salute during the Parade. This is *the* day of the year for the Chelsea Pensioners, and also an impressive occasion for spectators.

The Royal Hospital was founded in 1682, when King Charles II commissioned Sir Christopher Wren to design the elegant building which still stands today. It was not completed and opened, however, until 1692, by which time the Founder was dead and William and Mary occupied the throne. Tradition long prevailed that it was Nell Gwyn who drew the King's attention to the plight of the old soldiers and persuaded him to found the Hospital. In fairly recent years, however, this story has been torn to shreds. Credit for the foundation does stem, without dispute, from the interest of Charles II, who was well aware of the needs of the old soldiers of his day – but King Charles, with the best will in the world, was short of cash; and here enters the second man to play a notable part in the foundation of the Chelsea Hospital. This was Stephen Fox, later Sir Stephen Fox and Paymaster General. At that time he was a Treasury Commissioner and his job was to collect money and to pay the Army. For so doing he received a commission on every pound received, and in the course of time he accumulated a considerable sum of money. He felt, most creditably, that something should be done for the veterans of the Army with this money, and he used it to purchase the site of a partly completed theological college in Chelsea owned by the Royal Society; in addition, one day's pay was deducted annually from all ranks of the Army. This deduction continued for 100 years, and with the funds raised the Royal Hospital was built and maintained.

In recent versions of the Hospital's history, therefore, Nell Gwyn quietly bows out – which is sad, for it was a good story and one for which the Chelsea Pensioners had great affection. Who knows, Nell Gwyn probably *did* use her influence on behalf of the veteran soldiers, for with her humble origin she was in a better position than most in the King's confidence to bring the full story of their destitution to his notice. These veterans were then known as 'emerited soldiers', a term which, roughly translated, means deserving. The almshouses were full of them and they were given licences to beg – a sad and undignified end for an old soldier who had spent his life fighting for his country. The poet Francis Quarles (1592–1644) earlier drew attention to their fate in the following lines:

> *Our God and soldiers we like adore,*
> *When at the brink of ruin, not before.*
> *After deliverance both alike requited,*
> *Our God forgotten and our soldiers slighted.*

This was surely a state of affairs which Nell Gwyn would have tried to alleviate. A copy of a painting in the National Gallery, always believed to depict her, used to hang in a place of honour in the Great Hall of the Hospital – but today her portrait as well as her story has succumbed to the critics. Art experts declared that this portrait depicted Katherine Sedley, mistress of James II – so down came the portrait, and in its place was raised a portrayal of Sir Christopher Wren, whose role in the erection of the Hospital cannot be challenged. And since debunking is a popular modern hobby, it has even been said that Nell Gwyn's only association with the Royal Hospital was when her mother got drunk and, on falling into the ditch in Pimlico Road just outside the Hospital, was drowned.

The Chelsea Pensioners, if given their correct title, are referred to as In-Pensioners, a custom which dates from 1692 when the

Hospital was first opened and there were too many needy old soldiers for the accommodation available. Many were placed on Out-Pension, and some of them formed into Invalid Companies, being employed on Guard and other duties. Each Company was commanded by a Captain, and some time after the Royal Hospital was occupied a few of these Captains of Invalid Companies were admitted to the Royal Hospital. This accounts for the fact that the In-Pensioners are organised to this day into six Companies, each commanded by a Captain of Invalids.

An interesting custom among the In-Pensioners is that within the precincts of the Royal Hospital they still wear their old Regimental badges on their caps, even though some of the Regiments they represent were disbanded 40 or 50 years ago. When walking outside the precincts, however, the Pensioners wear a cap bearing the letters RH. When the Royal Hospital was first occupied in 1692 the In-Pensioners all had their old Regimental uniforms. This caused confusion, so the Hospital was allowed to adopt the present uniform of scarlet and blue. The familiar red coats are only worn in summer. The Royal Hospital, having been built on the site of a theological college, was for many years called Chelsea College, and to this day the In-Pensioners have the letters RCI on their uniform buttons. Various opinions have been expressed on their meaning – that they stand for Royal College of Invalids, or for Royal Chelsea Invalids, or for the Royal Company of Invalids.

Many are the 'characters' who have spent their last days in the Royal Hospital. One In-Pensioner, who died some years ago, had been Head Groom to three Viceroys of India. Another notable In-Pensioner was William Hiseland, famous for longevity – he married when over 100 years old and died in 1732 at the age of 112. He is buried in the Hospital's old graveyard, where also lies the woman soldier, Hannah Snell. She fought so valiantly that, when her sex was discovered and she was removed from the Army, they gave her a pension of six pence per day (later increased to one shilling) and allowed her to wear In-Pensioners uniform. She died in 1792 and was buried among the old soldiers with whom she had fought.

The In-Pensioners are today superbly well cared for, a state of affairs which would have delighted King Charles II, Sir Stephen

Fox, Sir Christopher Wren – and Nell Gwyn. As far as Sir Christopher Wren is concerned, he showed quite remarkable imagination and thoughtfulness in 1682, when a soldier was not considered to be of much consequence, in designing individual berths for the In-Pensioners instead of herding them into great barn-like dormitories. To each of the old soldiers this little room, with its own front door, represents home.

To qualify as an In-Pensioner it is necessary to have been a regular soldier, to have an Army pension for long service or disability, to be of good character, and to have 'no women encumbrances'.

In addition to Founder's Day (in late May or early June) two other ceremonies take place at the Royal Hospital, both in December. One is Presentation of the Australian Cake. Each State of Australia takes its turn in presenting the Royal Hospital with a cake, nearly always in the form of a map of Australia. The ceremony is held in the Great Hall and the Agents General of the States of Australia attend. The cake is cut by the oldest In-Pensioner with the Regimental Sergeant Major's sword, and each In-Pensioner receives a bottle of beer to accompany the cake. The other December custom is the Cheese Ceremony, when English cheeses are presented to the Royal Hospital. Again, the oldest In-Pensioner cuts the cheese with the Regimental Sergeant Major's Sword. This custom, which lapsed for many years, dates back to the early days of the Royal Hospital.

CHAPTER FIVE

Parliament

The seat of government in this country is the Palace of Westminster, the title which includes both Houses of Parliament and Westminster Hall. Edward the Confessor built his Palace and Minster beside the River Thames during the years leading up to the Norman Conquest of 1066, and of the eleventh-century buildings the splendid and historic Westminster Hall survives. This Hall was an addition to Edward the Confessor's royal residence, built by the Conqueror's son, William Rufus, and reconstructed by Richard II 300 years later. From this reconstruction dates the majestic hammer-beam roof, whose beams, with their angel embellishment, have looked down on the rise and fall of kings – on the magnificent coronation banquets of former times, on the scene when Edward II and Richard II were deposed, and when Charles I was condemned to death.

In early times the King's Council met wherever the monarch resided, and between the reigns of Edward the Confessor and Henry VIII the Palace of Westminster was the principal royal residence and home of England's Parliament. Henry VIII showed preference, as a residence, for his other inherited and acquired palaces, but the home of Parliament has always remained the Palace of Westminster.

The Lord Great Chamberlain still holds office as Keeper of the Royal Palace of Westminster, an hereditary appointment which, through failure of the original male line, is now shared by the three families of Cholmondeley, Ancaster and Carrington, all of direct descent. Once an office of considerable power, its responsibilities are today much reduced following the arrangement, by agreement, that each House should have more control over its separate parts of the Palace of Westminster. The Lord Great Chamberlain's robe is indicative of his hereditary role, for it consists of scarlet Court Dress incorporating the gold key emblem which denotes the key of the Palace of Westminster. It is an actual golden key which hangs at the back of his robe. The hereditary office of the Lord Great Chamberlain is not to be confused with that of the Lord Chamberlain of the Household, whose appointment by the Sovereign is non-hereditary.

In the early life of the Commons, meetings were held in either the Chapter House or the Refectory of Westminster Abbey, and then, following Dissolution of the Monasteries by Henry VIII, in St Stephen's Chapel. A massive fire in 1834 destroyed most of the old Palace, leaving as survivors (in addition to Westminster Hall) the Jewel Tower, the Cloisters and Crypt of St Stephen's Chapel. The rebuilding of the Palace of Westminster, with its Victorian Gothic towers and pinnacles and ebullient interior ornamentation, was the combined achievement of Sir Charles Barry and Augustus Pugin.

Originally the King's Council was composed of men of power and noble birth, both ecclesiastical and temporal, and it was not until the Civil War of the thirteenth century that Simon de Montfort, during his year of power (1264–5), first summoned to Parliament representatives from widespread communities and towns, enabling them to express their views and influence the government of the land. Thus Parliament as we know it began to emerge, and in the fourteenth century there developed a separate body, forerunner of today's House of Commons. It grew steadily in strength – a prime source of this strength being its power to extract money from the pockets of the people. To this day the Commons has retained the often unenviable task of controlling Britain's finances and taxes.

The power and privilege of the Commons was defied by two Kings. James I, in 1621, contested their claim to complete freedom in dealing with matters of grievance or policy, and he went so far as to wrench out the pages in the Commons Journal which recorded this claim. His son, Charles I, carried defiance still further, with tragic results. Guided by his unswerving belief in the Divine Right of Kings, Charles I defied Parliament at a time when his policies and theirs were widely opposed. It was John Pym, dedicated advocate of freedom of Parliamentary rule by strictly lawful means, who brought matters to a head with the Grand Remonstrance, which he laid before the Commons in November 1641. After long debate, it was adopted. Cromwell is recorded as saying, 'Had it been rejected I would have sold tomorrow all I possess and left England for ever'. There must have been many, in the years that followed, who wished that he had done so.

Charles I regarded the Grand Remonstrance as treason. He determined to arrest the five Members most closely associated with its introduction, and his messenger duly appeared at the Bar of the House of Commons, demanding the surrender of Pym, Hampden, Hazlerigg, Holles and Strode. He was received coldly and retired with his mission unfulfilled. The next day the King, in angry mood, set out for the Commons, determined to carry out the arrests himself. He was accompanied by his nephew the Elector Palatine (elder brother of Prince Rupert of the Rhine) and by an armed band of supporters who rallied to his side. But the five Members had been warned, and when the King reached the Commons (in St Stephen's Chapel) they were already making their escape by river. The King demanded to be told their destination, but he was met with the silent opposition of the House, followed by the historic reply of the Speaker, William Lenthall: 'I have neither eyes to see, nor tongue to speak in this place, but as this House is pleased to direct me'.

'Tis no matter', was the King's angry response. 'I think my eyes are as good as another's'.

As he left, his passage through the House was accompanied by murmurs and mutterings of disapproval, and the words 'Privilege, Privilege' were pronounced by many a Member.

The next day Charles I indulged in an equally unwise affront to the traditional liberty of the City of London, where the five Members had sought refuge. He entered Guildhall and demanded that they be surrendered; but the Sheriffs ignored the writs for their arrest, and with the words 'Privilege, Privilege' again ringing in his ears he left the City boundaries. The sparks kindled by this famous episode were soon to blaze into the Civil War, the executioner's block, and the Interregnum of Oliver Cromwell.

Since the attempted arrest of the five Members no Sovereign has stepped within the House of Commons – if one excepts King George VI's visit in 1950 to view the rebuilt Chamber of the House after war-time destruction.

Following the interregnum of Puritan rule a joyous welcome was extended to Charles ii in 1660. But the Stuarts, despite their personal charm, possessed a fatal strain of wilfulness and lack of wisdom which was their undoing. The following reign, that of James ii, ended in flight and the introduction of the blend of Constitutional Monarchy and Parliamentary rule which is so successful today. The Declaration of Rights, acknowledging the supremacy of Parliamenary law, was accepted in 1689 by William of Orange and Mary, daughter of the exiled James ii, and it was on these terms that they ascended the throne as William iii and Mary ii.

During 700 years of Parliamentary rule a vast heritage of ceremonies and customs has accumulated in the Houses of Parliament, and the House of Lords is the scene of the most important Parliamentary ceremony of the year, the State Opening of Parliament. This usually takes place early in November. It is a splendid occasion, for which the Queen sets out from Buckingham Palace in the Irish State Coach accompanied by the Duke of Edinburgh; the Crown (as related on p. 66) precedes her from the Palace in its own carriage.

At Westminster the Queen is received by the Earl Marshal, the Lord Great Chamberlain, and other Great Officers of State, and after proceeding to the Robing Room to assume her Parliament Robe and the Imperial State Crown, she walks in procession to the throne in the Chamber of the House of Lords. The Consort and the Prince of Wales occupy places in the alcoves on either side of the throne, and the latter, as heir to the throne, is on the Queen's right-hand side. At the State Opening of Parliament the traditional Wool-sack (from which the Lord Chancellor presides during sessions of the House of Lords) relinquishes its prominent position and the Sovereign enthroned becomes the sole focal point of the ceremony.

When the Queen has taken her place upon the throne the moment comes for the entry of the Commons. The Lord Great Chamberlain raises his wand, which is the sign that he has received the Queen's command for the Commons to be summoned and the Queen's Messenger, the Gentleman Usher of the Black Rod, sets out for the door which leads to the Commons. This is where a traditional ritual takes place which serves as a reminder of the abuse of privilege in the attempted arrest of the five Members. As Black Rod approaches the door the Serjeant at Arms closes it with a slam, whereupon Black Rod knocks three times upon the door with his rod. The Serjeant at Arms opens the grill, peers through, and the Queen's Messenger requests admittance. On this request being granted by the Speaker the Serjeant at Arms opens the door and Black Rod enters to convey his message; then the Commons, led by the Speaker and the Serjeant at Arms bearing the Mace, proceed to the House of Lords.

On arrival of the Commons at the Bar of the House of Lords, the Queen reads the Most Gracious Speech. 'Reads' is the correct word, for this is not, as is well understood, her speech – the Sovereign never partaking in politics – but the elected Government's elaboration of policies and programme for the coming session of Parliament. One wonders, sometimes, how the Queen must feel if the contents of that speech are unpalatable. But it is the sheer presence and dignity of the Queen, and her ability to hold the loyalty of both the elected Party and the Opposition, that lends stability to the Goverment, whichever Party gains power.

There was one occasion on which the Most Gracious Speech proved almost unreadable and inaudible. This was at the State Opening of Parliament on 4 February 1836 – close to the end of William iv's life and two years after the fire of 1834 had destroyed the Houses of Parliament. The State Opening was held in the old Court of Requests (since demolished) and the dim lighting proved a severe handicap for the King's failing eyesight. I will quote a nine-teenth-century account of the incident: 'Most patiently and good-naturedly did he struggle with the task, often hesitating, sometimes mistaking, and at others correcting himself. On one occasion he stuck altogether, and after two or three ineffectual efforts to make out the word, he was obliged to give it up; when, turning to Lord Melbourne, who stood on his right hand, and looking him most significantly in the face, he said in a tone sufficiently loud to be audible in all parts of the House, "Eh! What is it?" Lord Melbourne having whispered the obstructing word, the King proceeded to toil through the speech; but by the time he got to about the middle, the librarian brought him two wax-lights, on which he suddenly paused; then raising his head, and looking at the Lords and Commons, he addressed them, on the spur of the moment, in a perfectly distinct voice, and without the least embarrassment or the mistake of a single word, in these terms: "My Lords and Gentlemen – I have hitherto not been able, from want of light, to read this speech in the way its importance deserves; but as lights are now brought me, I will read it again from the commencement, and in a way which, I trust, will command your attention". The King then again, though evidently fatigued by the difficulty of reading in the first instance, began at the beginning, and read through the speech in a manner which would have done credit to any professor of elocution'.

Today the scene in Sir Charles Barry's ornate Chamber of the House of Lords is brilliantly lit and a magnificent sight, with the Queen enthroned, other members of the Royal Family in attendance, and the Peers in all the splendour of their Parliament robes. When the ceremony is over and the throne is empty once more both Houses prepare for the subsequent debates on the Speech.

The symbolic Woolsack in the Lords owes its origin to the days when wool was the great source of England's wealth, and between the Woolsack and the Table of the House are two elongated Judges' Woolsacks, equally traditional. The Spiritual side of the House is on the right when viewed from the throne, the Temporal on the left. The Bishops' seats are the only ones in the House of Lords which are treated to arm-rests at the end of each row.

The Lord Chancellor faces the House from the Woolsack when the throne is empty, and the Mace is placed behind him on the Woolsack. His title is Lord High Chancellor of Great Britain, and this should either be given in full or reduced to Lord Chancellor, the latter version almost invariably being used. His role is a complex one for he is a Peer, a Member of the Cabinet (and therefore politically of the government party) and also head of the Judiciary. When presiding from the Woolsack he is *outside* the House, for the Woolsack itself is deemed to be outside the boundaries of the House of Lords. Therefore, when addressing the House as a Peer, the Lord Chancellor must take a few steps to the left to bring him into the House. Unlike the Speaker of the House of Commons, he has no power to keep order or to control debate in the House.

Although the power of the Commons has grown so vigorously over the centuries, the Lords occupy a powerful role in the government of the country. All Bills, with the exception of the Budget and other financial legislation, are passed to the Lords for debate and assent when they have passed their Third Reading in the Commons. Due consideration is given in the Commons to amendments made by the Lords, action is taken upon them, and only when the final assent of the Lords has been granted is the Bill submitted to the Queen for the Royal Assent. It then becomes an Act of Parliament. If, however, the Lords refuse assent to a Bill, the Commons, after delay of a year, can obtain its enactment. Although most Bills start their life in the Commons, they can begin in the Lords and quite a number do; they then go to the Commons for assent.

The Royal Assent is still conveyed in Norman French. Three versions are used, according to the category of the Bill: '*La Reyne remercie ses bons sujets, accepte leur benevolence, et ainsi le veult*' for Money Bills; the briefer '*La Reyne le veult*' for other Public Bills; and '*Soit fait comme il est désiré*' for Personal Bills.

The House of Lords, unlike the Commons, is also a Court of Justice and the final Court of Appeal in the land. When the House of Lords sits in this capacity the Peers are those who are referred to as the Law Lords. Of these, a certain number are known as the Lords of Appeal in Ordinary, but in addition there may sit the Lord Chancellor, a retired Lord Chancellor, and a member of the House who holds or has held certain judicial offices (such as, for example, a Judge of the High Court who happens to be a Peer). There are always Members of the House of Lords who are of high judicial standing, for since 1876 distinguished Judges and Barristers have been created Life Peers for this very purpose. Although the House of Lords is the final Court of Appeal in the Land, no citizen should think that he has a good opportunity of getting a judgment reversed by taking an Appeal to the House of Lords. An Appeal does not, in fact, go to the Lords unless it is a matter of complexity and real importance.

There is, as one might expect, greater dignity in all aspects of the House of Lords than in the often belligerent sittings of the Commons, and this is even apparent in the form of voting when divisions are taken. The vote in the Lords is conveyed by a gracious 'Content' or 'Not Content', whereas the Commons express themselves succinctly with 'Aye' or 'No'. The word 'division' is a strictly accurate one, for in both Houses the voters divide into the 'Content' or 'Not Content' and 'Aye' or 'No' Lobbies. The term 'Reading', as applied to a Bill, also originally meant exactly what it says, for its use stems from the days when printing was specialised and costly and the Bill was read aloud, copies not being available for circulation. In the Lords, at the commencement of each Parliamentary session, a parchment roll is prepared by the Clerk of the Parliaments, and Members sign this as they take the oath. In the House of Commons Members' names are merely entered in a book.

The introduction of a new Peer is an important ceremonial occasion in the House of Lords, and for this the Lord Chancellor, wearing Court Dress, black gown, full-bottomed wig and tricorne hat, takes his place on the Woolsack. The tricorne hat is worn throughout the whole ceremony. The newly-created Peer has two Supporters (who must be Peers sitting in the House by right of a Peerage of the same degree) and he is attended by Garter King of Arms and Black Rod. All are in full ceremonial robes and the new Peer and his Supporters carry black cocked hats. The Earl Marshal and the Lord Great Chamberlain may attend, but they rarely do so.

On reaching the Woolsack the new Peer receives his Peer's Patent from Garter King of Arms and then, kneeling on his right knee, he presents to the Lord Chancellor his Writ of Summons and Patent. This is read by the Reading Clerk, who administers the Oath of Allegiance, and the new Peer signs the Roll upon the Table of the House; Garter King of Arms then conducts him, with his Supporters, to his bench where they put on their cocked hats, sit, then rise and bow three times to the Lord Chancellor, uncovering at each bow and finally remaining uncovered. When the ceremony is over the procession reforms and passes to the Prince's Chamber – and the new Peer's life as a Member of the House of Lords has begun.

Much less formal is the introduction of a new Member in the House of Commons following a Bye-Election. He has two Sponsors, corresponding to the two Supporters in the House of Lords. Together they stand at the Bar of the House and then, when the Speaker has made the appropriate announcement, they proceed to the centre gangway, making the customary bows. The Sponsors resume their seats, the new Member advances to the Table to present the certificate confirming his election, after which he takes the oath, signs the Roll, and is presented to the Speaker by the Clerk. It is all very perfunctory in comparison with the ceremony in the House of Lords – and rightly so, for the Member of the Commons is only there so long as his constituents elect, whereas the honour bestowed upon a new Peer is for life.

Reference to the Bar of the House is often baffling to those who have never entered the Parliament buildings. It is, in both Houses, a very important element in Parliamentary life, and the point beyond which strangers may not pass. In the House of Lords it is a waist-high wooden barrier, located at the opposite end of the House to the Woolsack. Black Rod sits by the Bar, *outside* the House. He is the Messenger of the Sovereign and attends all sessions of the House of Lords. His office is neither hereditary nor political. It is always his task to carry the message to the Commons when they are summoned to the Lords, and each time the ritual is performed of the slammed door and the three knocks with his rod.

In the Commons the Bar correspondingly marks the boundary of the House at the end of the Chamber opposite the Speaker's Chair. It is only drawn across as an actual barrier when the Sheriffs, accompanied by the City Remembrancer, present a Petition on behalf of the City of London, or when an offender against the House is brought to the Bar for judgment. The Government benches are on the right when viewed from the Speaker's Chair and the Opposition on the left. No stranger may step upon the floor of the House, and the space between the Government and Opposition benches is a traditional two sword-lengths apart.

I have already mentioned that the Lord Chancellor, unlike the Speaker, lacks power to keep order or to control debate. Another important difference is that the Lord Chancellor, as a Member of the Cabinet, is speaking for the Government when he addresses the House – and as a Member of the elected Government his office as Lord Chancellor terminates if a General Election favours the Opposition. The Speaker of the House of Commons, on the other hand, is non-political once he has been elected to the Speaker's Chair, and being non-political he does not necessarily lose office on a change of government. It is by no means an invariable rule that the Party in power in the Commons will elect one of its Members, and if the Speaker already in office is prepared to carry on he will probably do so. He is, traditionally, totally unbiassed, and all Speakers most certainly do their utmost to discard their Party allegiance once they have been elected to the Speaker's Chair. The Speaker of the House of Commons only votes when a casting vote is required.

Two other appointments independent of Party change are the Clerk of the Parliaments (Senior Officer of the House of Lords) and the Clerk of the House of Commons (Senior Officer of the Commons). Both are appointed by the Sovereign.

In the Commons tradition plays its part in the election of a new Speaker. On the day of the election the House is not in session, there are no opening Prayers and the Mace rests on supports beneath the Table. Proceedings begin with Black Rod's three knocks on the door and a summons to attend in the House of Lords. Here the Commons receive instructions to elect a Speaker, and they return to the Commons to carry out this task. But with the Speaker's Chair empty, no one in the House is qualified to control discussions or verbally to invite a Member to speak. The Clerk of the House therefore presides in silence and conveys his wishes by pointing. This interlude of mime is not as complicated as it sounds, for the nominee as Speaker-Elect and his Mover and Seconder have been chosen in prior deliberation. The Clerk rises from the Table, points to the Mover and sits down. The Mover speaks, and the Seconder, having had the finger of the Clerk directed towards him, rises to make his speech. The Mover and Seconder lead the Speaker-Elect to the Chair, and from this honoured position he addresses the House. The Mace is placed on the Table.

But the House of Commons has not yet come fully to life, for the Speaker-Elect is not Speaker until the following day, when the Queen's approval is conveyed to the Commons by the Lord Chancellor in the House of Lords. The new Speaker then takes the oath, and the next day Members do the same, the afternoon being reached before all have been sworn. Then the vivid and sometimes virulent body of the Commons has come into being once more.

As I have made clear, the Lords and the Commons work more closely together than the general public often realises, and apart from proceedings which they share the Central Lobby is the meeting-place of both Houses – a kind of English Channel between the Lords and the Commons. Each House also has its Peers Lobby and Commons Lobby. A curious convention exists in both the Lords and the Commons that the other House shall not be mentioned by name; it is referred to as 'another place' – at least, that is the convention, but it is not invariably adhered to.

The day opens in each House with the respective processions of the Lord Chancellor and the Speaker. The former is preceded by the Mace Bearer and the Purse Bearer. The Speaker's procession comprises, in the main, his Trainbearer, the Serjeant at Arms and Chaplain. The Purse, which forms a notable element of the Lord Chancellor's procession owing to its rich armorial ornamentation, once served to carry the Great Seal of the Realm, but the Great Seal is no longer borne each day into the House of Lords. In both Houses the approach of the procession is announced by the Police Constables, who call 'Hats off, Stangers'. This command is, incidentally, addressed to male strangers; a group of schoolgirls was seen recently to whip off every hat on hearing the command – a nice gesture, but not actually necessary.

Each day the sitting starts with Prayers, conducted by one of the Bishops in the Lords and by the Speaker's Chaplain in the Commons. In both Houses the prayer is that Members shall lay aside all private interests, prejudices and partial affections in order that the public wealth, peace and tranquillity of the Realm may be maintained.

Both Houses sit, officially, from Monday to Friday. The Lords' sittings, however, are primarily from Tuesday to Thursday, whereas the Commons sit throughout the full span of Monday to Friday and often through the night as well. The indication that Parliament is sitting is the flag which flies over the Victoria Tower by day; at dusk the flag is lowered, and a light is switched on which gleams from the summit of the Big Ben clock tower, conveying the same message. When the House rises, this light is extinguished.

With the end of the sitting the cry 'Who goes home?' echoes through the Lobbies and corridors, being repeated round the building by the Police. This custom originated in the days of highwaymen and footpads, due to the greater safety of travelling in numbers when the homes of Members were reached by open fields and deserted lanes.

A final custom worthy of mention is snuff-taking in the Commons. Smoking is not allowed in the Chamber of either House, and it is a centuries-old custom that the House of Commons snuff-box be available for the use of Members. It is in the custody of the Principal Doorkeeper. The snuff-taking habits of the eighteenth century are by no means dead, and when, during the 1941 raid of the last war, the former snuff-box succumbed with the Chamber of the House of Commons, a new snuff-box was made, nostalgically, from some of the old woodwork rescued from the remains of Sir Charles Barry's Chamber.

17   *Westminster School's Pancake Greaze – The Cook takes aim.*

18   *Boys of Christ's Hospital – the St Matthew's Day procession.*

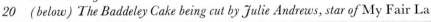

19 (above) *The Costermongers' Harvest Festival: the Pearly King, Queen and Prince of Tottenham at St Martin-in-the-Fields.*
20 (below) *The Baddeley Cake being cut by Julie Andrews, star of* My Fair La

CHAPTER SIX

The Law

The Inns of Court

London's Inns of Court, which lie to the north and south of Fleet Street, comprise an élite and secluded world, an isolated domain occupied by students of the law and those who practise it. Here are held lectures and examinations, and here is achieved the final qualification of being Called to the Bar. The atmosphere of the Inns of Court is serene, studious and completely remote in character from the traffic-dominated thoroughfares so close at hand.

The four Inns of Court are the Inner Temple, Middle Temple, Lincoln's Inn and Gray's Inn, and they are the universities of the law. Membership is composed of Benchers, barristers and students, and the whole area is riddled with chambers approached by enigmatic doorways and narrow staircases. The upper storeys are, in some instances, occupied by non-legal residents, and among the famous non-legal residents of the past were Charles Lamb, Oliver Goldsmith, Dr Johnson and William Makepeace Thackeray. Each Inn has its own Hall, Chapel and Library (the round Temple Church, consecrated in 1185, being shared by both the Inner and Middle Temple).

The seemingly changeless character of the Inns of Court is a fallacy, for the centuries have left a grim impact. The Great Fire of 1666, another fire in 1678, and the ravages of this century's two World Wars have swept much away, but damaged buildings have been restored, those destroyed have been replaced with skill and care, and the buildings which survived unscarred represent a treasured heritage of London's legal past. The curfew bell still rings each night at Gray's Inn (though silenced by war damage and during reconstruction) – a custom dating from the murder, in 1651, of the Under Treasurer, Thomas Tisdale, in his Chambers. After this grim deed the ruling was that 'the porter shall ridd the house of all suspicious persons and shutt the gates . . .' The custom of ringing the curfew bell also survives at Lincoln's Inn.

In addition to the four great Inns of Court there used to be Inns of Chancery as well. As far back as the records of Sir John Fortescue, Chief Justice in the reign of Henry VI (1422–61), there were listed the four Inns of Court and 10 Inns of Chancery. Originally the former were for the nobility and men of wealth, while the latter catered for students of the law of humbler means and for more elementary legal studies. Nevertheless, some of the great personalities of the law emerged from the Inns of Chancery, which eventually became attached, in groups, to the four parent Inns of Court. They then became extinct, the last to survive being Clifford's Inn, which ended its days in 1903. It was in the Hall of Clifford's Inn that the Judges met to settle boundaries after the Great Fire of 1666.

The title 'Inns of Court' stems from very early times when those who practised the law were of the King's Court. The word 'Inn' is used in its original meaning, denoting the residence of a noble or powerful family (as is still the custom in France, in the use of the word *hôtel*). In each case, therefore, the names are reminders of former occupiers. Lincoln's Inn is where the fourteenth-century Henry de Lacy, Earl of Lincoln, had his town residence; the Lords Grey de Wilton were occupants of the site of Gray's Inn in the distant past; and the Inner and Middle Temple were the home, from 1184 until 1312, of the Order of Knights Templars. When, in that year, the Order was dissolved, the Temple property was claimed by the Crown; subsequently it passed to the Knights Hospitallers of St John of Jerusalem, on whom the Pope had bestowed the forfeited estates of the Templars. In about 1338, during the reign of Edward II, the Temple area was leased to the professors of the law, and it has been legal territory ever since.

This original ownership was responsible for some of the disputes which arose between the Benchers and students of the Temple and the Corporation of the City of London. The City's claim was that the Temple fell within its area of jurisdiction, while the Inner and Middle Temple claimed that the ecclesiastical nature of the property made it subject to the protection of the Papal See and free of all other jurisdiction. Outbursts of strife resulted. The inflammatory symbol was the City Sword which the Lord Mayor was entitled to have carried upright within the boundaries of the City of London. The dispute came to a head in 1554 when the Lord Mayor, Sir John Lyon, was invited to the Reader's Feast of John Prideaux of the Inner Temple. He arrived in state, his Swordbearer carrying the City Sword upright – at the sight of which the students took action and dragged it down.

But the most notable example of resistance in this connection occurred on 3 March 1669, during the reign of Charles II. The occasion was the Feast of the Lent Reader of the Inner Temple, Christopher Goodfellow, and among his guests was the Lord Mayor, Sir William Turner, together with some of the City Aldermen. This invitation was obviously fraught with danger, and the Reader knew that there would be trouble if the Lord Mayor insisted on asserting his right with the City Sword. Therefore he despatched, most diplomatically, a couple of spokesmen to request him to avoid using this source of contention – but the Lord Mayor's response was far from conciliatory. 'My service to your Reader' he replied. 'Tell him I will come and dine with him. I will bear up my Sword and see who dares take it down'.

The Lord Mayor, in this intransigent mood, duly arrived at the Inner Temple where the students, revolt boiling in their blood, only needed the sight of the upright City Sword to ignite them. They beat it down and attacked the Lord Mayor's attendants, forcing them to take flight. The Lord Mayor himself had to seek shelter in the Chambers of the Exchequer Auditor – a sorry defeat after his 'take it down who dare' challenge. The splendid Reader's Feast came nowhere near his lips, and after a while he decided on retreat; but in the Temple Cloisters his attackers again descended upon him, and he was compelled to regain the sanctuary of the Exchequer Auditor's Chambers. At last the prospect of the Reader's dinner lured the students away, and the Lord Mayor made his escape to undisputed territory. According to Samuel Pepys's description of this fracas, 'My Lord Mayor did retreat out of the Temple by stealth, with his Sword up', which indicates that he made his escape with some semblance of glory. When the Lord Mayor placed his complaint before Charles II the case went before the King's Council and the Inner Temple was ably defended by Sir Heneage Finch. The King then ruled that the privileges of the Temple must first be tried in a Court of Law – at which point the Lord Mayor decided to let the matter drop.

In the Great Fire of London of 1666 the Middle Temple was more fortunate than the Inner Temple, yet the Middle Temple suffered most of the two from the less publicised fire 12 years later, on 26 January 1678. It was during this fire that the Lord Mayor and City Sheriffs, showing an admirable sense of forgiveness for past indignities, came to the Temple to offer assistance. But again the City Sword was borne upright into the Temple area, and once more the students of the Inner Temple, ignoring the crisis of the fire, refused to allow the symbol of City jurisdiction to pass. They beat down the sword as before, and the Lord Mayor, his good intentions shunned, was forced to seek cover in a near-by tavern. It is said that he soothed his injured feelings by stopping and dismissing a party of City fire-fighters which was on its way to the blaze – a rather nasty though understandable revenge, if the tale is true.

The Inns of Court, as the resort of sons of noble and wealthy citizens, used to be noted for the splendour and richness of their masques, revels and other festivities. In 1594, during the reign of Queen Elizabeth I, Shakespeare's *Comedy of Errors* is believed to have had its first performance in the Hall of Gray's Inn; and in 1601 Shakespeare's *Twelfth Night* was performed in the Hall of the Middle Temple – possibly by Shakespeare's own Company, with the poet himself in one of the roles. The Middle Temple Hall, which dates from 1570, is almost unique in having been continuously used for the same secular purpose since it was built. It is the custom for each Treasurer's coat of arms or name to be emblazoned on the walls in Hall, and these galleries commemorating past Treasurers have reached impressive proportions.

The last of the famous Inns of Court revels was held in 1733 in the Hall of the Inner Temple. At this the traditional custom was followed whereby the Lord Chancellor, the Masters, Judges and Benchers formed a ring and circulated, hand in hand, three times around the hearth (the fireplace formerly being in the centre of the

Hall). A singer provided the musical accompaniment for this stately perambulation, and it is interesting to note that he was none other than Tony Aston, the member of Thomas Doggett's strolling players whose personal description of the founder of Doggett's Coat and Badge Race I have quoted (p. 94).

Today revelry plays little part in the life of the Inns of Court and the gatherings on Grand Day are affairs of dignity. Dinners are convivial yet formal, all attending in gowns and, in three of the Inns, the procedure is strictly governed by precedence. The Masters of the Bench enter in procession and take their seats on the dais, the seating of the barristers and students being graded according to seniority. Only in the Middle Temple is a less formal convention adopted, ignoring order of seniority.

In each of the Inns of Court the assumption reigns that all know each other and introductions are unnecessary. Occasionally there is lack of recognition, and introduction is then veiled behind such phrases as, 'I think you have met Smith'. (Barristers, incidentally, address each other only by the surname.)

The toasts on Grand Day in each Term are traditional. At Gray's Inn, where Queen Elizabeth i is especially revered, the toast is always to 'The glorious, pious and immortal memory of good Queen Bess'. At this Inn, too, a ceremony of great antiquity takes place at each Grand Day Dinner – the Presentation of the Cup of Hippocras. When all have assembled and Grace has been said, the Masters of the Bench leave the dais and take their seats in the body of the Hall, whereupon each Bencher and Guest is passed a dish of toast and bread cubes and a Loving Cup containing spiced wine. This wine is prepared from a secret recipe which has been passed down from one Butler to another. It is often suggested that the ceremony is of Sacramental origin, but this is considered unlikely, for Holy Communion would never have been celebrated with spiced wine, and there is no record of Holy Communion having been celebrated in Hall instead of in the Chapel.* The ceremony was taking place as early as 1552, for it is described in Wriothesley's *Tudor Chronicles*.

---

* *The Presentation of the Cup of Hippocras* by Master the Hon. Mr Justice Hilbery. *Graya*, No. 44, 1956.

Toasts at Gray's Inn take the form that the senior member of the mess, with his glass filled, names each of the members in order of seniority and drinks the toast. He is followed by other members in order of seniority, each naming the other members and drinking to them collectively. When barristers toast barristers the names are without prefix, but when toasting students (or when students toast any member of the Society) 'Mr' or a title, if applicable, is used.

At Lincoln's Inn it is the custom (as in the Navy) for members to remain seated during the Loyal Toast, and the story behind this royal dispensation is that on one of the occasions when Charles II dined at the Inn some of the members were a little unsteady. The adaptable monarch not only suggested that they remain seated but granted the right to do so in perpetuity. The Middle Temple has the same privilege, but this had its origin with the Sailor King, William IV, and was probably on the Naval principle.

Horns are still blown in the Temple as a summons to mess in Hall, a custom first mentioned in the Inner Temple records of 1621, 'That the horne may blowe for dinner before eleaven of the clocke and before sixe for supper and that as sone as there are three messes in the hall then the Buttlers to serve out; and att the serving of the first messe an houre glasse to bee sett uppe and such gentlemen as come not into the hall before itt bee runne out to dine and suppe in the parliament house'. The men who served at table in the Temple used to be called Panniermen, and it has been suggested that this name derived from the *Panarii* who served the Knights Templars. It was the Pannierman who blew the horn for dinner, a task now carried out at both of the Inns by one of the porters. At Lincoln's Inn the Pannierman existed from about 1483 until 1848, when replaced by the Usher of the Hall.

The Pannierman also, in times past, announced the commencement of the Moot, or mock trial, which was so excellent an exercise for students of the law in pleading or defending a case. These mock trials were of very early origin, and in announcing their commencement the Pannierman would call: 'A pleader, a pleader, mes Seigneurs touts . . .' Gray's Inn was especially famed for its Moots in the past. The Inns of Court Moots, for a time discontinued, are now revived.

Among the most intriguing features for visitors to the Inns of Court are the frequently displayed armorial devices. These are: the Winged Horse Pegasus (Inner Temple); the Paschal Lamb and Banner, usually referred to as the Lamb and Flag (Middle Temple); the Lion Rampant (Lincoln's Inn); the Griffin Segreant (Gray's Inn). The Inner Temple's Pegasus emblem is also represented in Gray's Inn and the Griffin in the Inner Temple – a symbol of amity between the two Inns since the sixteenth century.

In the Temple the Lamb and Flag and Pegasus devices are encountered in especial abundance, beside doors, over doors, above gateways, and – if you raise your eyes skywards – at the top of drainpipes. In the reign of Queen Elizabeth I the Winged Horse, Pegasus, was already the device of the Inner Temple, whereas the first record of the Middle Temple's Lamb and Flag occurs in the seventeenth century (reign of Charles I) – 'an Agnus Dei trotting, carrying a staff bearing a Cross and streamer'.* The arms of the Temple Societies have never, as far as can be traced, received legal sanction, but the Lamb and Flag device was recognised and engraved as the arms of the Middle Temple by Sir William Dugdale (then Norroy, and later Garter King of Arms) in *Origines Juridiciales* in 1666. It was the Lamb and Flag and the Winged Horse which inspired an eighteenth-century versifier to chalk the following much-quoted lines on one of the Temple gates:

> *As by the Templars' holds you go,*
> *The Horse and Lamb display'd,*
> *In emblematic figures shew*
> *The merits of their trade.*
>
> *That Clients may infer from thence*
> *How just is their profession,*
> *The LAMB sets forth their INNOCENCE,*
> *The Horse their EXPEDITION.*
>
> *Oh happy Britons! happy Isle!*
> *Let foreign Nations say,*
> *Where you get Justice without guile,*
> *And Law without delay!*

* Brere MS. *c.* 1638.

This effusion served as a challenge to an embittered contemporary, who penned the less frequently quoted response:

> *Deluded men, these holds forego,*
> *Nor trust such cunning elves;*
> *These artful emblems tend to shew*
> *Their CLIENTS, not THEMSELVES.*
>
> *'Tis all a trick; these are all shams*
> *By which they mean to cheat you;*
> *But have a care, for you're the LAMBS,*
> *And they the Wolves that eat you.*
>
> *Nor let the thoughts of 'no delay'*
> *To these their Courts misguide you;*
> *'Tis you're the shewy HORSE, and they*
> *The Jockies that will ride you.*

In addition to the devices in the Inns of Court, plaques bearing dates and coats of arms or initials are seen. This is due to the convention that whenever a new building is erected these emblems of the Treasurer in office shall be placed on the frontage. If construction occupies several years, then more than one Treasurer is commemorated, for this is an annual appointment.

The Benchers' meetings have their individual titles in each Inn of Court: in the Temple they are Parliaments; in Lincoln's Inn, Councils; in Gray's Inn, Pensions.

When the law student has passed his examinations and has dined in Hall the required number of times, he is 'Called to the Bar'. This used to be marked by numerous formalities, but today the newly qualified barrister merely signs the Publication of Call Book. Later, a barrister who earns distinction in the profession may achieve the status of Queen's Counsel. This is referred to as 'taking silk', an expression which derives from the change to a silk instead of alpaca or 'stuff' gown. After receiving the Queen's Patent the new QC presents himself at the Royal Courts of Justice, where he is called upon to 'enter within the Bar'. This means that he will sit, in future, in the row of seats reserved for Queen's Counsel.

The Law Courts

The Royal Courts of Justice are located midway between the southern Inns of Court (Inner and Middle Temple) and those north of the Strand and High Holborn (Lincoln's Inn and Gray's Inn). From early times until erection of the massive nineteenth-century edifice in the Strand, the Law Courts were established in the Palace of Westminster (with the exception, from the early eighteenth century, of the Court of Chancery which sat in the Old Hall in Lincoln's Inn). In Westminster Hall the great timber roof looked down on an extraordinary mixture of legal proceedings, which progressed amidst the turmoil of shopkeepers' stalls and milling crowds, for the public were allowed unrestrained access. Such unsavoury characters as the straw-men once loitered near the Law Courts, a wisp of straw in the shoe indicating that they were willing to be hired as false witnesses.

An anecdote in *Gentleman's Magazine* in 1737 recalls Peter the Great's visit to Westminster Hall during his sojourn in England. The Russian Tsar seemed mystified by the legal proceedings in progress and asked who the people were in wigs and black gowns. On being told that they were lawyers he appeared astonished and exclaimed 'Lawyers! Why, I have but two in my whole dominions, and I believe I shall hang one of them the moment I get home'.

In 1882 the Royal Courts of Justice moved to the Strand, and by contrast with the congested hurly-burly of earlier days they acquired premises which offer them, according to their own official guide, 1,000 rooms in the main building alone and three and a half miles of corridors.

The opening of the new legal year provides an opportunity for the public, by means of the Judges' Procession at Westminster, to see the dignitaries of the law in their full ceremonial robes. This takes place on 1 October (or the first weekday in October if the date falls at the weekend), and after Divine Service in Westminster Abbey the learned procession sets out for the House of Lords, to be regaled with the Lord Chancellor's 'Breakfast'. The Lord Chancellor with his Mace-bearer, Pursebearer and Trainbearer is at the head, followed by the

Lord Chief Justice, the Master of the Rolls, and Her Majesty's Judges. Distinctive among them is the Admiralty Marshal, bearing on his shoulder the Silver Oar Mace of Admiralty. And foremost of all in this procession of the greatest legal personalities in the land walks a man clad in a plain black uniform and peaked hat. He carries a silver-mounted staff – successor of the 'tipped staff' from which his ancient office gained its name – for he is, in fact, the Tipstaff, whose task is to arrest all who are accused of Contempt of Court. The Judges later return to the Royal Courts of Justice in the Strand, and the new law year has then opened.

At the 'Court of Admiralty', which sits in the Royal Courts of Justice and is technically part of the Queen's Bench Division, the Silver Oar Mace lies on brackets before the Judge. The cases which come up for judgment in this Court involve ships at sea in oceans far remote from these shores, and here the wisdom and advice of the Elder Brethren of Trinity House is a factor in decisions. The Admiralty Court handles cases concerning shipping of all nations, and the Admiralty Marshal's officers have power to board any ship and prevent it from sailing when a claim is pending. They can, in fact, arrest the ship, and when this happens the writ is affixed to the mast.

The Central Criminal Court

This is known the world over as the Old Bailey and it is located within the square mile of the City of London. The building stands on the site of Newgate Prison in which, prior to erection of the first Old Bailey in 1539, many of the trials were held. Fear of Judge and Jury contracting the dreaded gaol fever caused the sixteenth-century Old Bailey to be built, but the peril was not eliminated, for a couple of centuries later the fever was conveyed by Newgate prisoners on trial. The Lord Mayor, two Judges, an Alderman, a Sheriff, and about 50 others died, and two years later another Lord Mayor succumbed. The practice was then introduced of strewing herbs, believed to ward off infection; in addition, posies of flowers were carried by the Judges, their fragrance helping to conceal the smell of the prisoners' unwashed bodies. Posies are still carried, by tradition, on two days of each month from May to September, and when the Lord Mayor attends the first two days of each session at the Old Bailey he, too, carries a posy during this summer period.

Among many famous trials in the history of the Old Bailey one needs to be singled out – the trial of the Quakers William Penn and William Mead in 1670, for preaching to an unlawful assembly in Gracechurch Street. The Jury of 12 men refused to give a verdict against them, for which they were themselves imprisoned – four suffering months in gaol under conditions of great hardship. But they stood their ground and established a principle of the law which has held good ever since – that no Jury may be punished for its verdict.

Quit Rent Ceremonies

Royal Courts of Justice (usually second half of October)

Quit rents are token rents – something that most of us would like to qualify for. They represent a gift of land or property granted long ago and usually marking the Sovereign's appreciation for services to the nation. The meaning of the title is that on rendering the required service the tenant goes quit and free.

Two London quit rent ceremonies involve such unusual obligations as the splitting of faggots with a hatchet and the counting of horseshoes and nails. Both have been carried out faithfully over a period of more than 700 years. One concerns land called 'The Moors' in Shropshire, and the other land on the north side of the Strand, between the churches of St Clement Danes and St Mary-le-Strand, and incorporating the site of Australia House.

'The Moors', in the parish of Eardington, near Bridgnorth, Shropshire, became the subject of a quit rent rendered to the Crown in 1211, during the reign of King John. In the Roll of Shropshire Sergeantries of 1211 is the entry: 'Richard the Medlar holds one virgate of land and renders for the same at the Feast of St Michael two knives'. Later in the same century the Great Roll of the Exchequer records, 'One Nicholas de Mora paid at the Exchequer two knives, one good and one very bad, for certain land which he holds of the King in capite in Mora'. In 1254 the Hundred Rolls for Shropshire record 'Mora Nicholas Le Medlar holds a virgate of land in capite of the Crown, rendering at the Exchequer two knives to cut a hazel rod, the other to bend in green cheese; and that no other service be rendered for the land'. (A virgate of land was about 20–30 acres – a quarter of an hide, and in the Domesday Book of 1086 an hide was the amount of land which a team of oxen could plough in the course of one year).

In 1521 a licence granted alienation of this land held of the Crown at an annual rent of 'two knives of which one must be of such strength that a Knight, if one be present, or someone else if no Knight be present, holds a hazel stick of one year's age and of one cubit's length and striking the said stick with a weak knife, the said weak knife makes little or no mark on the stick, and a good knife, at the first stroke on the stick, ought to cut it in half, which service must be done in the Middle of the Exchequer in the presence of the Treasurer and Barons each year on the day following Michaelmas'. This alienation of the land was in favour of John Heweson, John Costwyth, Richard Gresham, John Gresham, William Locke and Richard Austen, two of whom, Sir Richard and Sir John Gresham, became Lord Mayor of London in 1537 and 1547. They may have held the land henceforth on behalf of their Livery Company or on behalf of the City of London, for since that time the City of London has been responsible for the quit rent. It has been rendered with only one break – during the Interregnum of the Cromwellian Commonwealth.

For centuries a hatchet and a billhook have represented the good and the bad knives – possibly due to the fact that in medieval times all small cutting instruments were referred to as knives. The hazel stick has become a bunch of hazel twigs.

The ceremony takes place before the Queen's Remembrancer in the Royal Courts of Justice. It opens with the following proclamation:

'Tenants and occupiers of a piece of waste ground called "The Moors" in the County of Salop, come forth and do your service'.

The Comptroller and City Solicitor, representing the tenants and occupiers, thereupon 'comes forth' and proceeds to wield the billhook, 'the very bad knife'. It makes a poor impression on the faggots, so he takes the hatchet and brings it down with a resounding crash, dealing with the hazel twigs most successfully. The Queen's Remembrancer, who has been watching carefully, pronounces the words, 'Good service', and the City Solicitor retires to his seat in the Court.

The second quit rent ceremony was first referred to in the Great Roll of the Exchequer in 1235, six horseshoes and 61 nails representing payment by Walter Le Brun Le Mareshal for a plot of land for a smithy in the Parish of St Clement Danes. This quit rent was rendered annually by Walter Le Brun and afterwards by his son John Le Brun, then by his grandson, another Walter Le Brun. Extra land was bestowed for enlargement of the smithy by Henry III in 1261. The Knights Templars occupied the neighbouring Temple area, where their tilting and jousting ground lay, and for this the services of the Le Brun smithy would have been well placed. It was finally destroyed during riots in the reign of Richard II, but although the actual smithy had disappeared the Corporation of the City of London continued to render the quit rent.

The form that the ceremony takes today is still the rendering of six horseshoes and 61 nails, and they are the same ones used throughout the centuries – of formidable size, having belonged to the massive Flemish horses used on the jousting ground and made to protrude beyond the hoof. These jousting horses played an important role in the contest for they were trained to fight with the forefeet, and all six of the horseshoes rendered in this ceremony are for the forefeet. Again a proclamation opens the ceremony:

'Tenants and occupiers of a certain tenement called "The Forge" in the Parish of St Clement Danes in Greater London come forth and do your service'.

The City Solicitor rises once more, and this time his task is lengthier and more lugubrious. One by one he counts the six great jousting horseshoes, and then, with infinite patience, he counts slowly and deliberately each nail, holding it up for the Queen's Remembrancer and all in the Court to see, until number 61 is reached.

'Good number' says the Queen's Remembrancer approvingly, and on this note of commendation the City Solicitor returns once more to his seat. The hatchet and billhook, the ancient horseshoes and the nails, all are taken away into safe custody, and the fragments of hazel twigs are gathered up.

The Court of Exchequer, before whom in earlier times these quit rents were rendered, was first established by William the Conqueror, and combined both the Treasury and the Law Courts. Today the sole surviving office of the Court of Exchequer is that of the Queen's Remembrancer, and since 1859 the quit rents have been rendered to him in the Royal Courts of Justice.

CHAPTER SEVEN

Schools

The Pancake Greaze at Westminster School

(Shrove Tuesday)

A long-established custom at Westminster School is the Shrove Tuesday Pancake Greaze, which involves tossing an outsize pancake over a lofty bar, followed by a wild scramble to capture the largest fragment. The word 'greaze' is old Westminster School slang for a squeezing together or a scrimmage. The first recorded reference to the custom was made by Jeremy Bentham, the jurist and social reformer who was at Westminster School from 1755–60, but the Greaze is believed to be of much greater antiquity than this. At one time (possibly until the first decade or so of the nineteenth century) the old Schoolroom was divided by a curtain hanging from an iron bar near the ceiling. Eventually the curtain disappeared – but the iron bar remained, for without it the Shrove Tuesday Greaze could not be held, and that would be unthinkable. The School Cook must toss the pancake over the bar, and then comes the Greaze – an all-out scrum aimed at capturing the largest remnant of mangled pancake. The reward is the traditional 'golden guinea'. Formerly the whole school took part in the scramble, and then it was a massive tussle; but in 1885 the then Head Master, Dr W. G. Rutherford, reduced the number of competitors to one boy from each form. This, at the time, was deemed a retrograde step, likely to reduce the Greaze to a mild affray; but no one who has watched the present-day scrum could describe it as mild.

The Greaze usually takes place at 11 am on Shrove Tuesday. The non-participating boys gather in the Hall, forming a solid mass of youthful humanity penned behind a barrier at the platform end.

The noise and excitement are tremendous. Meanwhile, the scales are carried in for weighing the pancake fragments. Then, dead on time, the procession enters – the Beadle with his mace, leading the Dean's Verger, the Dean of Westminster, and the Head Master, the Cook and the selected team of competitors. All eyes are on the Cook, for in his hand he clasps a frying pan containing a solid round chunk of pancake – sufficiently weighty to make the throw possible over the lofty bar.

The competitors range in size from large to small, and when I saw the Greaze in 1973 some of the boys had dressed in school 'rag' mood, with mock bloodstained bandages producing an intimidating appearance. The Cook, clutching the frying pan, took aim for the distant bar. The competitors waited, tense and ready to spring – and total silence fell in the great Hall. Then, suddenly, the frying pan was swung and up soared the pancake – up and (good throw!) over the bar. At once pandemonium broke loose and the boys became a scrambling mass of bodies where the pancake fell. Then, from the whirl of legs and arms, several triumphant figures emerged, each clutching a piece of mangled pancake. These were duly weighed and the winner, overcome with glory, was presented with the award. Finally, the Dean 'begged a play' (part of the tradition of the Pancake Greaze) – which means that he requested a holiday for the boys. The Head Master gave his consent, the holiday was declared for the following day, and then everyone dispersed. The Pancake Greaze was over for another year.

In this custom of the Westminster School Pancake Greaze the man who earns our sympathy is the Cook. What if he misses the bar? It seems that today a misthrow would be treated with tolerance, but in earlier times it was a disastrous blunder, for no golden guinea was allocated. In 1865 the Cook missed the bar for the third time running, and this was altogether beyond toleration. The boys took revenge by pelting him with books, and the Cook, goaded beyond endurance, flung his frying pan at them, injuring one boy's head.

The ambition used to be to capture the pancake in its entirety, but this was almost impossible to achieve. Once, however, history was made by George Francis Wells, and the incident was recorded by Captain F. Markham in his *Recollections of a Town Boy at West-*

21   *Harvest of the Sea Thanksgiving Service.*
22   *Distribution after the Oranges and Lemons Service.*

23   *Grimaldi Commemoration Service.*   24   *The Butterworth Charity.*

25   *The Farthing Bundles of Fern Street*

minster (1849–55). George Wells was a small and delicate boy, unlikely to have had much ambition to achieve this remarkable feat. It was a case of glory being thrust upon him. He was standing in the front line of boys when the pancake came hurtling in his direction; then a push from behind felled him to the floor and, amazing discovery, the precious pancake was lying beneath him. Swiftly he concealed it within his waistcoat, wriggled out of the fray, and waited quietly until the Greaze was over. Everyone was mystified. What on earth could have happened to the pancake? Gradually the company dispersed, and only later, when there was no chance of his trophy being seized, did George Wells unbutton his waistcoat and claim his golden guinea. This small boy, obviously destined to win his way through life by strategy rather than muscle, later became Rector of Boxford, Berkshire.

The Pancake Greaze is always a big day for Westminster School, and in 1919 it became a royal day too, when King George V and Queen Mary witnessed the custom, accompanied by the Prince of Wales and the Duke of York (later King Edward VIII and King George VI). The winner received the Dean's guinea and an additional guinea, presented personally by the King.

During the last war Westminster School was evacuated to Herefordshire, returning in 1945 to buildings severely damaged by the fire and blast of the heavy air raid of May 1941. The great Schoolroom was roofless, but the vital pancake bar survived. So in March 1946 the first post-war Pancake Greaze was held in circumstances unlikely to be repeated; with the ground thick with snow, the pancake was tossed over the faithful bar which had withstood the blast and bombs of war.

The King Edward VI Foundations

The Bridewell Service and King Edward VI's School

On the second Tuesday in March an annual service of dedication and thanksgiving is held in St Bride's Church, Fleet Street. It commemorates the foundation of Bridewell Royal Hospital by King Edward VI on 26 June 1553 – a foundation today represented by

King Edward's School at Witley, Surrey. The Lord Mayor attends
in state, and the church is crammed with the boys and girls of the
school. This service recalls the dream of Edward VI and Bishop
Ridley that a reformatory and school might be established in the
Royal Palace of Bridewell – a dream which developed nightmare
qualities when the premises became part-prison and part-school, but
which now achieves everything that the King and Bishop could have
hoped for, and more.

The Royal Palace of Bridewell once occupied an area beside the
River Fleet extending from Fleet Street to the River Thames at
Blackfriars. It was built by Henry VIII between 1512 and 1523 –
destruction by fire of much of the Palace of Westminster having made
a new royal residence desirable. It was a great, stolid palace of Tudor
brick, and here Henry VIII received the Papal Legate, Lorenzo
Campeggio, during negotiations for divorce from his first Queen,
Catherine of Aragon. All who are familiar with Shakespeare's *Henry
VIII* will be conscious of the Palace of Bridewell as the setting for
Act III. As time went by, however, Bridewell became distasteful to
Henry VIII, for the tidal River Fleet which flowed past his windows
was increasingly despoiled by filth from habitations upstream; and
acquisition of the Palace of Whitehall and of Hampton Court en-
abled him, henceforth, to show preference for scenes more fair than
Bridewell with its offensively polluted stream.

In May 1552 Nicholas Ridley, Bishop of London, pleaded with
King Edward VI that the desolate palace might be used for the
accommodation of London's homeless – for Henry VIII's Dissolution
of the Monasteries had created a multitude of poverty-stricken and
sick people who had formerly been cared for by the religious houses.
The City authorities had been greatly concerned with this problem,
and they had already been successful in acquiring St Bartholomew's
in 1544 for care of the sick (enabling continuation of the service
performed since its monastic foundation as a hospital by Rahere in
1123), and later the Greyfriars Monastery, renamed Christ's Hospital, was founded as a school for poor boys; St Thomas's Hospital
and Bethlem Hospital were established for the sick and mentally
afflicted.

As a result of this plea Edward VI sought Bishop Ridley's advice on the measures to be taken, and similarly he called upon the services of the Lord Mayor, Sir Richard Dobbs; and in his eagerness to support the project the King offered to allocate to Bridewell the land and rents, chattels, furniture and linen of the Savoy Hospital. The young King, desperately ill, completed the arrangements by Charter on 26 June 1553 – and by 6 July 1553 he was dead.

The transformation of Bridewell to its new purpose was embarked upon with high hopes. The Long Gallery of the erstwhile palace became a workshop, and here the homeless men and women of the City were set to work on spinning, weaving and hemp beating. The children wore a distinctive uniform, and the boys were apprenticed to such crafts as weaving, shoemaking and tailoring. Some did well in later life and the system justified itself.

But alas for good intentions – as time went by Bridewell Hospital sank very far below the ideals of its foundation. Replicas, known by the multiple title of Bridewells, were established in other parts of the country, and they became a means of forcing work from vagrant and idle persons rather than aid for the poor. Gradually use as a prison usurped the original purpose as a training centre and reformatory. Worst of all, in the 1630s a whipping post was set up in Bridewell with accommodation for spectators, and wrongdoers of both sexes, often brought from outside for punishment, provided sport for the gaping eyes of the public. Bridewell was also used for detention of religious prisoners – Roman Catholics, Quakers, and the Congregational sect known as Separatists; and during the Civil War Royalist prisoners were held within its walls. Then came the Great Fire of 1666, leaving the building severely damaged.

Bridewell was rebuilt, however, and during this period of a second chance there were again high hopes for its future. Samuel Pepys, much concerned in the whole project of training homeless children for useful employment, became one of the Governors, and by 1673 the apprentices were back. A truly educational element now developed, with reading and writing included in the instruction, previously restricted to crafts. This was the good side of the rebuilt Bridewell. The bad side was that it still served as a prison alongside the School of Apprentices, the prison inmates consisting of prostitutes, pickpockets and recalcitrant apprentices sentenced to hard labour.

Then, in the early years of the nineteenth century, opposition grew to the policy of educating apprentices under the same roof with vagrants and prostitutes, and in 1830 the Bridewell apprentices were removed to St George's Fields where a 'House of Occupation' was opened to provide a general and industrial education for boys and girls. In 1855 the prison closed and Bridewell's revenues were devoted entirely to educational work. From 1860 King Edward's School at Witley provided education for boys while the girls' school remained at St George's Fields, eventually combining to form a single co-educational school at Witley.

Today, for the annual Service of Dedication and Thanksgiving at St Bride's, the choir is composed of the boys and girls from Witley. The Head Boy, as a member of the Guild of St Bride, reads the Lesson; and later in the service the Head Master reads the Thanksgiving. The Bridewell Mace, symbol of the School Commission, is offered on behalf of the Lord Mayor; blessing is pronounced upon King Edward's School; and after the Dedication the prayer of Bishop Nicholas Ridley is said – the prayer of the kindly Bishop of London who, despite his good deeds, was burnt at the stake in October 1555, during the blood-besmirched reign of Queen Mary I. The sight of the bright and intelligent young people from the school at Witley who attend this service would be the best possible reward for Edward VI, whose creation of Bridewell Hospital was almost a dying act, and for the martyred Bishop who had envisaged so excellent and valuable a role for the great, empty palace.

Christ's Hospital – London Processions and Other Customs
St Matthew's Day Procession, 21 September

Twice yearly the scholars of Christ's Hospital walk through the City of London in procession, the boys immediately recognisable in their Tudor-design uniforms of blue ankle-length coat and yellow stockings. This uniform has earned for them the title of 'the Blue Coat boys' – a title which the school itself rejects, for there were other blue coat schools but only one Christ's Hospital. A Christ's Hospital boy is correctly referred to as 'a CH boy', and an old boy of the school is an 'Old Blue'.

This famous school, among whose Old Blues can be numbered

Samuel Taylor Coleridge, Charles Lamb and Leigh Hunt, was part of the Royal Foundation of Edward VI's Charter of 1553 which also brought about the foundation of Bridewell. Henry VIII, following Dissolution of the Monasteries, had granted to the Corporation of the City of London the land and buildings of the Grey Friars at Newgate for charitable use. The Corporation allocated them to the newly-formed school, and for over 400 years the City of London's interest and association with Christ's Hospital has remained very close.

The story of the foundation of Christ's Hospital was the same as Bridewell, its benefactors being Edward VI, Bishop Ridley, the Lord Mayor, Aldermen and individual men of wealth of the City of London. Unlike the Bridewell, however, Christ's Hospital was always a school for necessitous children – never a house of correction, and it never had to share its premises with a prison. Both these royal foundations have now left London, the Christ's Hospital boys being established at Horsham in Sussex and the girls at Hertford, just as the Bridewell Hospital became King Edward's School at Witley, Surrey. In the seventeenth century Samuel Pepys became actively concerned with Christ's Hospital as Governor (just as he was also a Governor of Bridewell), and his interest resulted in establishment of the Royal Mathematical School within the original foundation by Charles II's Charter of 1673. It was as Secretary to the Admiralty that Samuel Pepys urged the plan for this second royal foundation, the aim being to supply sailors for the Navy and Merchant Service by maintaining 40 boys for instruction in the 'Art of Arithmatique and Navigacon'. After training they were examined by the Elder Brethren of Trinity House and then, if successful, they went to sea.

The benevolent interest in Christ's Hospital which has always been shown by the City of London is epitomised by the St Matthew's Day celebrations. That day (21 September) is when, by Act of Parliament, the list of Governors of the Royal Hospitals must be handed to the Lord Mayor. On St Matthew's Day, therefore, the school used to congregate at Christ Church, Newgate Street, for this purpose and for the annual church service which accompanied the handing over of the list. Today the pupils converge on London from Horsham and

Hertford and congregate in the Church of St Sepulchre-without-Newgate, Holborn Viaduct, for the service (Christ Church having been burnt out during the last war). The service is attended by the Lord Mayor, and the sermon is preached by a distinguished Old Blue. Afterwards the Christ's Hospital boys and girls (well over 300 in number, selected from the total of 1,100 pupils at Horsham and Hertford) march through the City streets, led by the school band. Their destination is the Mansion House, where each receives a money gift composed of coins fresh from the Mint and personally presented by the Lord Mayor. Then a buffet meal awaits them in the Egyptian Hall of the Mansion House.

The other occasion when Christ's Hospital boys walk in procession in the City is on Corpus Christi Day, the election day of the Skinners, the Livery Company whose interest in the school has provided regular scholarships throughout the years. After the election has taken place at Skinners' Hall, Dowgate Street, the Skinners' procession forms, led by the Christ's Hospital boys, and all walk to the Church of St Mary Aldermary to attend the election day service – everyone, including the boys, carrying the traditional posy of fresh garden flowers.

A reminder of the school's royal associations is the right of a Christ's Hospital scholar to present an Address to the Sovereign during the State Visit to the City of London which follows accession to the throne. Queen Mary I did not like the 'blewe boys' whose school had been founded by her Protestant half-brother, and when she found them awaiting her with their Address, on a stage specially set up at Aldgate by the school's Governors, she 'cast hir eie an other waie'.* The Protestant Queen Elizabeth I graciously received their Address at Temple Bar in 1559 – and later Sovereigns have been equally gracious, including Queen Elizabeth II.

A private benefactor of Christ's Hospital introduced a curious custom in the eighteenth century which has survived at the school to this day. James St Amand, who died in 1754, left a bequest whose terms required that a portrait of his grandfather, John St Amand, be produced and shown at every first Court of Governors held after 1

* John Howes MS.

January each year, and that the section of the will relating to the portrait be 'audibly and publickly read at the same time in open Court'. Each January, therefore, at the meeting of the Court of Governors, this part of the will is duly read and the portrait of John St Amand (a miniature set in gold) is passed round for inspection and appreciation.

Sir John Cass School – Red Feather Day

(On or near 20 February)

Within sight of Aldgate Pump is the Sir John Cass School, and beside it is the Church of St Botolph Without Aldgate. Here, on or near 20 February, staff and pupils from the school may be seen making their way into the church, each wearing a scarlet plume in cap or lapel. This is a custom which has prevailed for over two and a half centuries, and the story behind it is this.

Sir John Cass was born on 20 February 1661 in East Smithfield, and he was baptised in the Church of St Botolph Without Aldgate (predecessor of the present church, rebuilt in 1744). On reaching maturity he prospered, became Master of two City Livery Companies, the Carpenters and the Skinners, and was Alderman of the Ward of Portsoken, Sheriff of London, Member of Parliament for the City. With all his success he had one over-riding ambition – to found a school in the Aldgate area of his birth. In 1710 he built the school within the churchyard of St Botolph Without Aldgate, and eight years later he died, on 5 July 1718.

When Sir John Cass felt that death was near his most pressing concern was that his wife should have adequate finances to maintain the school during her lifetime, and that it should be sufficiently endowed to ensure continuation after her death. Tradition has it that while he was signing the will which made this possible he had a pulmonary haemorrhage and died; but he had succeeded in signing the will, although the quill pen grasped in his hand was stained scarlet with his blood. The custom of wearing a scarlet plume for his memorial service was adopted as a token of homage, and has been continued ever since.

Today, after the Memorial Service is over, the Governors of the Sir John Cass Foundation, the Managers of the School, the staff and guests, all proceed to the boardroom and pledge the Founder's memory in a Loving Cup. The toast is drunk in hot mulled wine, made from a recipe believed to date from Sir John Cass's day. And the plumes, readers may like to know, are turkey quills (a little smaller than a swan's quill), dyed scarlet.

CHAPTER EIGHT

The Church

I have already described under *Monarchy* the ceremonial of the Coronation, together with the Maundy distributions and the Royal Epiphany Service; the memorial services for Remembrance Sunday, Trafalgar Day and the Battle of Britain are included under *The Services*, and the Bridewell Service under *Schools*. In this section, therefore, I shall concentrate on some of the most interesting and unusual of London's commemorative and thanksgiving services not already mentioned, together with some words on the bells and bellringers of the City of London.

Bells, 'Pearlies', and Oranges and Lemons

Most children know the nursery rhyme about London's bells, but in case any reader has missed this bit of childhood lore, these are the words:

> *'Oranges and lemons', say the bells of St Clements,*
> *'You owe me five farthings', say the bells of St Martins',*
> *'When will you pay me?' say the bells of Old Bailey,*
> *'When I grow rich', say the bells of Shoreditch,*
> *'When will that be?' say the bells of Stepney,*
> *'I do not know', says the Great Bell of Bow.*

It is a deep-rooted tradition that no Londoner can claim to be a true Cockney unless born within the sound of Bow Bells. Therefore the 'Pearly' costermongers, who are the Cockney royalty, regard the Church of St Mary-le-Bow in Cheapside with an hereditary eye, and they helped to raise funds for restoration of the Great Bell of Bow and the rest of the church's bells after destruction during the last war. Fragments of the bells were buried beneath the crypt; then, after the war, they were dug up, melted down, and the bells re-cast; Prince Philip, Duke of Edinburgh, set them pealing once more on 20 December 1961. The first child to be baptised in the rebuilt church was the grandson of a Pearly King and Queen.

The Pearlies' own church, St Mary Magdalene in the Old Kent Road, was also lost during an air raid of the last war, and the October Costermongers' Harvest Festival was transferred to St Martin-in-the-Fields, Trafalgar Square – the second of the nursery rhyme churches, whose bells announce so accusingly, 'You owe me five farthings'. This Harvest Festival Service is the best occasion in the year for seeing a gathering of the Pearlies in all their splendour. London's costermongers, with their barrows and stalls of fruit and vegetables, have been part of the London scene as far back as medieval times, but their famous costume (suits, dresses and hats thickly encrusted with pearl buttons, while brightly-coloured ostrich plumes decorate the hats of the women) only came into being during the last two decades of the nineteenth century. In the records of St Pancras there is an interesting account of a nineteenth-century Coster funeral which reads:

'*14 January 1884. Mary Robinson, aged 71, Queen of the Costers, buried at St Pancras Cemetery.* She was an apple stall woman, and is said to have amassed over £50,000 by loans to the costermongers of Somers Town and Islington. Her funeral from Upper Bennington Street, Islington, was a remarkable sight. She was carried to her grave by four men in clean white smocks and, by her directions, twenty-four young women wearing violet dresses, and hats with feathers, attended her funeral, which was followed by hundreds of costers and others, many probably in the hope of participating in the beer, tobacco, and long clay pipes provided by the expenditure of ten guineas especially bequeathed for that purpose'.

Not all Coster Kings and Queens amass a fortune like the apple woman, Mary Robinson. They are a hard-working and far from wealthy section of the community who have, nevertheless, been assiduous in collecting funds for those in greater need than themselves. The Pearlies always take part in the Lord Mayor's Show, and they participate in many London functions for which charity is the aim. Their costumes are a masterpiece of industry and craftsmanship, and the men are as ingenious in design and as handy with the needle as the women.

For the October Harvest Festival Service at St Martin-in-the-Fields the Pearlies arrive in goodly number – a fantastic company of Pearly Kings, Queens, Princes and Princesses of the various London boroughs, their costumes gleaming with hundreds and thousands of pearl buttons. Their titles are hereditary. The Harvest Festival Service is warm-hearted and cheerful in mood, well in keeping with the character of the Pearlies. The altar and pulpit are arrayed with the fruits of the earth, a Pearly King reads one of the Lessons, and the congregation sings with vigour the familiar hymns of the harvest season.

Equally charming in quite a different way is the annual Oranges and Lemons Service at St Clement Danes Church in the Strand (on a weekday in the second half of March). 'Oranges and lemons, say the bells of St Clements', and on this day at St Clement's Church there are great piles of oranges and lemons in the porch awaiting distribution to the children. Traditionally the service is a legacy of the days when barges brought cargoes of citrus fruits from the ships moored downriver, and these were unloaded on the Thames shore south of the church.

On this Oranges and Lemons Day the children participate in the service at almost every stage. They read the Lessons, sometimes singly and sometimes in unison, and they recite the Oranges and Lemons nursery rhyme. They sing such well-loved hymns as *All Things Bright and Beautiful*, and finally they perform the Oranges and Lemons melody on handbells – at least, they did at the 1974 service which I attended. By the end of the service the tables bearing their loads of oranges and lemons have been moved from the porch to the outside of the church, and here they are distributed to the children as they leave.

To turn from bells to bell-ringers, the Ancient Society of College Youths have been ringing the City of London's bells for more than three centuries. The Society was founded on 5 November 1637 and its structure is roughly based on the same lines as a Livery Company. The first Master was Lord Brereton, and, like the Livery Companies, there is an annual 'Feast'. All members being assembled (usually 200 or more), the Toastmaster announces, 'Gentlemen, receive your Master', whereupon the Master enters, escorted by the Senior and Junior Stewards, the former carrying the Society's silver mace of 1762. Toasts are to 'The memory of the Masters of 300, 200 and 100 years ago' and 'The Youths of 50 and more years' membership'. During the evening a touch of *Stedman Cinques* is rung on handbells – a complicated 'change' composed by Fabian Stedman, Master of the Society in 1684.

Change-ringing first developed as a secular sport rather than a purely ecclesiastical practice (the bells which summoned the congregation to church were not at that time change-ringing but chimes). The ringers attracted to the activity were mainly from the Universities of Oxford and Cambridge, and from the Inns of Court. They adopted names such as *The Schollers of Cheapside, The Norwich Scholars* – and *The College Youths*. The Ancient part of the College Youths' title stemmed from an eighteenth-century split into two groups, the Ancients and the Juniors, and the title remained unchanged after the breakaway group of Juniors had ceased to exist.

The College Youths have rung Bow Bells since 1637, and at St Paul's Cathedral they ring for the Sunday services throughout the year. At St Lawrence Jewry they are responsible for the joyful peals which announce the Admission of the new Lord Mayor at Guildhall. And on special occasions they ring at St Michael's, Cornhill, and St Giles, Cripplegate.

The St Paul's ring consists of 12 bells with 12 ringers operating the ropes and usually about three men in reserve. Each ringer stands on an individual wooden platform in order to avoid the tail-end of the rope getting entangled with his feet, a danger only likely in St Paul's Cathedral owing to the great size of the bells.

The bell-ringers' tower at St Paul's is the North West Tower, and its walls are covered with plaques announcing peal-ringing records achieved over the years by the Ancient Society of College Youths. In the neighbouring South West Tower are two famous bells used for tolling, not for change-ringing. One is Great Tom, which tolls the hour and also tolls when there is a death in the Royal Family or on the death of the Archbishop of Canterbury, the Bishop of London, the Dean of St Paul's, or the Lord Mayor of London should he die in office. Great Tom is not, however, the largest bell. This is Great Paul, sounded daily at 1 pm – the largest bell in the country and weighing 16 tons 14 cwt.

The members of the Ancient Society of College Youths are neither ancient nor youths – they are just an excellent age for the highly-skilled role they fulfil and for clambering on foot to the top of belfries. They assemble unfailingly to ensure that the bells ring out over the roofs of the City, and they also undertake rigorous 'peal ringing' marathons (ringing 5,000 or more changes consecutively). The Reverend R. H. Barham refers to the Society in 'The Wedding Day' in his *Ingoldsby Legends* (1840):

> *Spare we to tell of the smiling and sighing,*
> *The shaking of hands, the embracing, and crying,*
> *The toot-toot-toot of the tabour and flute,*
> *Of the white-wigg'd Vicar's prolong'd salute,*
> *Or of how the blithe 'College Youths' – rather old stagers,*
> *Accustom'd, for years, to pull bell-ropes for wagers –*
> *Rang, faster than ever, their triple-bob-Majors.*

On a more sombre note, I must mention the bell which resides in a glass case in the Church of St Sepulchre (opposite the Old Bailey). This was the Execution Bell, provided under the Bequest of Robert Dowe in 1605 – a handbell which was rung at midnight outside the condemned cell of the neighbouring Newgate Prison, at which time the following verse was recited to the prisoners whose lives were so shortly to be terminated:

> *All you that in the condemned hole do lie,*
> *Prepare you, for tomorrow you shall die,*
> *Watch all, and pray; the hour is drawing near*
> *That you before the Almighty must appear.*
> *Examine well yourselves, in time repent,*
> *That you may not to eternal flames be sent,*
> *And when St Sepulchre's Bell in the morning tolls*
> *The Lord have mercy on your souls.*

In the south wall of the church can be seen the top of a closed-in archway. This was once the entrance to the underground passage by which the bellman made his midnight journey to the door of the condemned cell in Newgate Prison.

King Charles I – Memorial Services and Ceremonies

In the *Parliament* section King Charles I is seen through the eyes of the House of Commons of his day – as the apostle of the Divine Right of Kings and the opponent of Parliamentary privilege. In the memorial services and gatherings of loyalists on and around 30 January, anniversary of his execution in 1649, the other side of the picture is presented. The King, despite errors of judgment, has earned the veneration of many (since his canonisation in the 1660s) and unanimous respect for his dignity in captivity and at his Trial, for loyalty to his beliefs and courage on the day of execution. Oliver Cromwell is remembered, in general, as a dour man who brought misery to countless homes and irreparable damage to many a cathedral and fine old church – who foisted upon the land a cheerless Puritan régime which the majority of the people liked less and less as the years went by.

On the day of execution King Charles, after receiving Holy Communion in the Chapel Royal of St James's Palace, walked across the park to the Palace of Whitehall. On arrival, he retired to his former bedchamber for a period of prayer, and here he was joined by ecclesiastics of the Puritan faith – whose companionship in prayer he declined, remarking that they had so often prayed against him that he would not have them pray with him in his extremity. On reaching the scaffold the King's courage did not waver. 'I go from a corruptible to an incorruptible crown' were his words, and after making a declaration of his faith he laid his head on the block. The poet Andrew Marvell, although a Puritan, has written the best-known lines on the subject of this tragic scene:

> *He nothing common did or mean*
> *Upon that memorable scene;*
> *But with his keener eye*
> *The axe's edge did try;*

Nor called the gods, with vulgar spite
To vindicate his helpless right;
But bowed his comely head
Down, as upon a bed.

And so King Charles I, with the dignity of sovereignty and the charm inherent in all the Stuarts, passed into history. Oliver Cromwell, victor of the Civil War and the Puritan cause, suffered far greater indignities as time went by. He died on 3 September 1658 and was buried, after being embalmed, on 26 September – the coffin, as described by John Evelyn, bearing his effigy 'in royal robes and crowned with a crown, sceptre and globe like a king, but it was the joyfullest funeral I ever saw; for there were none that cried but dogs'. Within less than a year after the 1660 Restoration of the Monarchy the body of Oliver Cromwell suffered such indignity that posterity is appalled – especially when one realises that this was not the act of hooligans but of Parliament. Oliver Cromwell's body was disinterred, drawn on a sledge to Tyburn, and there, with the exhumed bodies of Ireton and Bradshaw, was hanged. At dusk, the grim relic was cut down, the head removed, the body buried beneath the gallows and the head hoisted later on a spike on the roof of Westminster Hall – an aptly chosen place of retribution, for here the Trial of Charles I took place and here he was condemned to death.

It is difficult, today, for any writer not to sit slightly on the fence when discussing the place of these two men, Sovereign and Protector, in the eyes of posterity. Oliver Cromwell's tragedy is that vastly different honours might have been accorded to him had the Civil War been a conflict against a foreign enemy. Then his great qualities of military leadership might have placed his name, alongside those of Marlborough, Wellington and Nelson, among the heroes of our history. But this will never be. King Charles, on the other hand, has been accorded a scale of veneration which would undoubtedly have surprised him and even the most devoted of his contemporaries. Societies have been founded in his name, among them the Society of King Charles the Martyr, established in 1894. Its purpose, in addition to veneration of the Martyr King, was dissent over the 1859 removal from the Prayer Book of the three State

Services, included in 1662, which commemorated the death of Charles I, the Restoration of the Monarchy, and failure of the Gunpowder Plot.

Today a number of commemorative services are held each 30 January under the auspices of the Society of King Charles the Martyr. The first is a short service at the Banqueting House in White-hall, scene of the execution, and here a wreath is hung beneath the King's bust which surmounts the north-west door; full commem-orative services are then held in the Churches of St Mary-le-Strand and St Margaret Pattens.

Following the foundation of the Society of King Charles the Martyr another society with similar aims came into being, the Royal Martyr Church Union; their annual service is usually held in the Church of St Martin-in-the-Fields, Trafalgar Square, followed by a procession and another short service beside the King's statue at the Trafalgar Square end of Whitehall. The Royal Stuart Society also hold a wreath-laying service at the statue. Advance details of all these commemorative services and wreath-laying ceremonies are published in *The Church Times*.

The Pepys Commemoration Service

St Olave's Church, Hart Street (on or near 26 May)

'I to church, and there, beyond expectation, find our seat, and all the church crammed . . .' So wrote Samuel Pepys on 20 January 1667 in the Diary which has provided the most amusing, vivid and widely read account of life in the seventeenth century to come down to posterity. The perennial readability of this Diary ensures that Samuel Pepys's Church of St Olave, Hart Street, is each year 'all the church crammed' for the Pepys Commemoration Service – but not 'beyond expectation', for this is one of London's most imaginative and nostalgic commemoration services.

St Olave's is among the few City churches to survive the Great Fire of 1666 and the destruction of the last war. It suffered blast and fire in 1941, but the arcades remained almost intact, and in the excellent restoration much of the old stone was used. Therefore, when attending the Pepys Commemoration Service, one sits beneath the arches upon which Pepys's eyes rested 300 years ago. The seating has altered, however, the galleries having been removed in the nineteenth century. Pepys sat in a gallery on the south side of the church reserved for the Navy Office, for in 1660 he was Clerk of the Acts to the Navy and later became Secretary of the Admiralty.

Although a regular churchgoer, Pepys was not always the most attentive member of the congregation. The gallery was a good viewpoint and we find in his Diary, 'To church where, God forgive me, I did most of the time gaze on the fine milliner's wife in Fenchurch Street'; and again, 'To church, where Mr Mills preached, but I know not how. I slept most of the sermon'.

St Olave's is full of Pepysian memories. His wife, Elizabeth, died in 1669 – over 30 years before her husband's death. The monument which commemorates her was chosen with great care by Samuel, who loved her dearly despite his roving eye, and he had the monument placed where he could always see it from the Navy Office gallery.

In the graveyard of St Olave's many plague victims were buried – far too many to be wholesome to Samuel Pepys's way of thinking. Above the entrance gateway in Seething Lane is the skull and crossbones ornamentation which caused Charles Dickens to christen this 'the churchyard of St Ghastly Grim' in *The Uncommercial Traveller*.

Samuel Pepys died on 26 May 1703 and was buried in the same vault as his wife, beneath the communion rail of St Olave's. In the middle aisle his brother Tom (who also figures in the Diary) was buried in 1664. The Commemoration Service is always held as near as possible to the anniversary of the diarist's death, and usually the Lord Mayor attends to place a laurel wreath in front of his memorial. Also present are the Sheriffs, the Master and Wardens of the Clothworkers' Company, and the Elder Brethren of Trinity House. Pepys was appointed Master of Trinity House in 1676 and Master of the Clothworkers' Company in 1677; the Rector of St Olave's is Chaplain of the Clothworkers' Company. The music is entirely of the seventeenth century, and the address is usually given by a noted Pepys authority.

When I attended the Commemoration Service in 1973 the music

of Pepys's day included an anthem by John Blow composed for the coronation of James II; music by Matthew Locke, Composer in Ordinary to Charles II; and a song composed by Samuel Pepys himself for baritone solo and lute, sung to a new arrangement for baritone with organ accompaniment. The address was by Robert Latham, Fellow and Pepys Librarian of Magdalene College, Cambridge. A final nostalgic touch – the old pewter plates used for the collection were the same that were used in Pepys's day.

Stow Commemoration Service – Changing The Quill Ceremony

Church of St Andrew Undershaft, Leadenhall St (on or near 5 April)

The Church of St Andrew Undershaft is associated in the minds of all historians with John Stow (1525–1605), who worshipped here for many years and was buried within the church. Stow, whose famous *Survey of London* has been of inestimable value to later historians, was the son and grandson of a tailor. He was himself apprenticed, becoming a master tailor at the age of 24, and he followed this occupation for about 15 years. Thereafter he indulged his taste and genius for historical research. Having enriched posterity with the results of his labours, he ended his days in poverty, and King James I granted him, during the last two years of his life, a 'Licence to Beg', which enabled him to receive contributions from friends and admirers of his work. In recommending Stow's cause, the King added the words, 'having already in our own person and of our special grace begun the largesse for the example of others . . .' Nothing equivalent to a present-day old age pension existed in Stow's day, although he was awarded a pension by the Merchant Tailors' Company, of which he was a Freeman. Throughout the literary period of John Stow's life he must have sat long hours at his desk, studiously delving, researching and writing on the London of earlier times; and so he sits today – or rather, so sits the memorial figure on his tomb – with quill pen in hand and a look of deep meditation on his face.

It is the annual changing of this quill pen by the Lord Mayor of London that is the central ceremony of the Stow Commemoration

Service. An address is given, always by a distinguished historian, and then a procession forms and advances to the Stow Memorial. The historian has the task of removing the old quill pen and presenting the new one to the Lord Mayor, who then places it in the stone hand of John Stow's effigy.

The Church of St Andrew Undershaft gained its name from the lofty Maypole which once stood before the south door and rose higher than the tower of the church itself. After a May Day in 1517 when the apprentices rioted the Maypole was never again raised, but lay on hooks above the doorways in Shaft Alley. Then, early in Edward VI's reign, the Curate of the Church of St Katharine Cree declared it a pagan symbol, and the householders, fearing the 'idol' affixed to their homes, hauled it down, cut the shaft into pieces and burned it. So the Maypole was no more, and today even Shaft Alley has disappeared, for its site is occupied by the P & O building. But Stow sits in his north-east corner of the church, quill pen in hand. He seems to be meditating, as throughout his lifetime, on the loss of treasured scenes and the onslaught of change – the need to record all before, like the great Maypole of Shaft Alley, it is swept away.

The Florence Nightingale Commemoration Service

Westminster Abbey (on or near 12 May)

It is difficult to think of any woman who has contributed a greater share to the service of humanity than Florence Nightingale. Even so, a hundred years passed before the centenary of her departure for Scutari brought a national commemoration service into being. This she would not have resented, for she was reticent where personal publicity was concerned, and she was the last person to view herself in a saintly guise. Yet to the sick and wounded men of Scutari 'the Lady with the Lamp' was a saint indeed. At the commemoration service now held annually in Westminster Abbey the traditional lamp is carried to the High Altar, not only in memory of Florence Nightingale but also as an act of rededication of the nursing services to the ideals and standards which she instigated.

Florence Nightingale was born on 12 May 1820 and her childhood was spent in surroundings that would normally augur a life of wealth, comfort, culture and leisure. In early youth, however, she developed a fervent desire to nurse the sick and ease the sufferings of humanity – a desire which reached fulfilment when the year 1854 ushered in the Crimean War with its terrible record of inefficiency and mortality due to sickness and neglect in the military hospitals. In October 1854 Florence Nightingale with her team of 37 nurses left England and at Scutari set to work. Under appalling conditions she organised an efficient nursing service, installed diet kitchens and laundries, and provided recreation for the men in convalescence. In 1855 she toured the military hospitals of the Crimea, contracting a fever which nearly proved fatal. It was at Scutari, however, that her almost legendary reputation was born, for here she established the routine of her nocturnal tours of the hospital wards, her lamp held aloft to ensure that no soldier was lying in the darkness needing care.

For the rest of her days Florence Nightingale worked tirelessly in the cause of improved nursing, modernised hospitals, and the better understanding of hygiene and sanitation. The Nightingale School for the training of nurses was established at St Thomas's Hospital, and from the qualified nurses who emerged were selected those best fitted to start similar nurses' training schools, not only in other parts of this country but also in Australia and the USA. This systematic training, based on 'the Nightingale System', eventually spread far and wide. Honours were bestowed upon her in full measure during her last years, and when she died on 13 August 1910 Westminster Abbey was the offered place of burial. But she was laid to rest quietly in the family grave at East Wellow, near Romsey, Hampshire.

The commemorative service which honours her life of dedication takes place each May, the month when she set out for her tour of the military hospitals of the Crimea. The date is always fixed as near as possible to her date of birth, 12 May. The service commences with a procession which includes the Honorary Officers of the National Florence Nightingale Memorial Committee of Great Britain and Northern Ireland and also, representing the soldiers who were Florence Nightingale's first concern, the red-coated Pensioners from the Royal Hospital, Chelsea. During the service the lamp is carried from St George's Chapel to the Sanctuary by a Chief Nursing Officer escorted by Student and Pupil Nurses. It is then passed to a Ward Sister, then to a Staff Nurse, to the Sacrist, and finally to the Dean of Westminster, who places it on the High Altar.

The lamp brought to the Abbey is of traditional design, for the one believed to have been carried by Florence Nightingale at Scutari (of the camp lantern type, and now on loan to the National Army Museum at Chelsea) is too delicate and precious a relic to be used.

The Lion Sermon

St Katharine Cree Church, Leadenhall Street, EC3 (16 October)

This sermon represents a three-centuries-old expression of gratitude. Each year, on 16 October, the miraculous escape of Sir John Gayer from attack by a lion is commemorated in the Church of St Katharine Cree, and each year the Preacher re-tells the story.

Sir John Gayer was a West Country man who came to London in the 1620s to seek his fortune. His ambitions were well fulfilled, for he prospered and became a Sheriff of the City in 1635. He established the Levant Company, trading in the Near East, and it was on one of his journeys with merchandise of the Levant Company that Sir John's escape from the lion took place. He became separated from the caravan as darkness fell, and he was left, in the silent loneliness of the desert, beneath the great expanse of the starlit sky. At least, he was left in silent loneliness until the silence was broken by a terrifying sound. It was the roar of a lion. Sir John was a man of habitual prayer, and he fell on his knees, praying to God that it might be His will to deliver him from the death which seemed so close. Then he lay down calmly to sleep. At dawn, when other members of the caravan found him, he was sleeping peacefully on the sands of the desert; and all around him were the footpads of the lion. It had stalked round and round the sleeping man during the long hours of night.

Sir John Gayer returned to England and continued to prosper, becoming Lord Mayor of London in 1647. But he never forgot the miracle in the desert, and he endeavoured to show his gratitude by

181

good deeds. He made generous gifts to Christ's Hospital, to various causes in Plymouth, and to the London church where he worshipped, St Katharine Cree, he made a bequest of money to be used among the poor of the parish – on condition that every year, on 16 October, the story of his miraculous deliverance from the lion be retold.

So the Lion Sermon continues to be preached each year on the anniversary of Sir John Gayer's night of peril. The last sermon, at the time of writing, was the 330th, and on that occasion a member of the Gayer family (Brigadier W. M. Gayer of Ditchling, Sussex) read the Lesson; it was, as may be anticipated, the story of Daniel in the lion's den. The Preacher, after the traditional repetition of the escape in the desert, devoted the theme of his sermon to 'Gratitude', the emotion which governed Sir John Gayer for the rest of his days.

Blessing of the Throats

St Etheldreda's Church, Ely Place (3 February)

On the Feast Day of St Blaise (3 February) the thirteenth-century crypt of St Etheldreda's Roman Catholic Church in Ely Place welcomes pilgrims for the Blessing of the Throats. Most are sufferers from diseases of the throat. All through the day they come, and at regular intervals of about 15 minutes the priest descends to the crypt to administer the blessing. As soon as his footsteps are heard on the stairs, the men and women who have been waiting come forward. In the priest's hands are two consecrated unlighted candles placed together in the form of a cross, and as he holds this against the throat of each person he pronounces the blessing of St Blaise.

St Blaise, Bishop of Cappadocia, was martyred in AD 316 during the persecution of the Christians initiated by Diocletian. His association with the Blessing of the Throats is due to the legend of his miraculous cure of a boy who was at the point of death with a fish-bone stuck in his throat. Legend also relates that during his imprisonment prior to martyrdom a woman came to his cell with a gift of candles, whereupon St Blaise pronounced that all who in future made him a similar offering would have his protection.

St Etheldreda's Church is the ancient Ely Chapel, sole survival of the days when the town residence of the Bishops of Ely occupied Ely Place and the present Hatton Garden area. In 1576 Sir Christopher Hatton, Lord Chancellor to Queen Elizabeth I, was granted a 21-year-lease of part of this episcopal property, including the garden and orchard, the rent being £10 per annum, a red rose and ten loads of hay. The Bishop ensured, however, that he and his successors might walk in the gardens and gather 20 bushels of roses each year.

The church is of interest as the first pre-Reformation church to be regained by the Roman Catholics in this country. Stained glass depicts the first martyrs of the Reformation, all five executed at Tyburn on 4 May 1535, and along the north and south walls are statues of later martyrs.

Ely Place, with its sedate houses and St Etheldreda's Church, is separated from the outer world of Holborn Circus by a Lodge; from this, until the outbreak of the last war, the Beadle would sally forth nightly to call the hour. The Beadle remains but his call is silenced – and it would be difficult today to imagine gathering 20 bushels of roses in the neighbourhood of Ely Place.

Harvest of the Sea Thanksgiving Service

Church of St Mary at Hill, EC3 (Sunday, first half October)

St Mary at Hill is a short street which leads Thameswards from Eastcheap, and the church which bears the same name as the street is approached by a narrow alleyway half-way down the hill; the main entrance is, in fact, in Lovat Lane, not in St Mary at Hill at all. At the foot of the hill is Billingsgate Market, whose site has been used as London's fish market since medieval times, and St Mary's is the Parish Church of Billingsgate.

Everything around here tends to be redolent of fish and fishermen, of sea or river or boats – especially in the early hours of the morning when fish predominates and Billingsgate comes alive while most of London sleeps. Near the bottom of St Mary at Hill Watermen's Hall creates a sudden architectural dignity, while the Livery Hall of the Fishmongers' Company is also near by, on the west side of London Bridge.

Around the church the smell of fish enters the very portals – especially on the occasion of the Harvest of the Sea Thanksgiving Service in October, when not only the smell but the fish itself is encountered within the entrance porch. A great slab occupies a good three-quarters of the porch area, and on this is laid out fish of every kind, from lobsters to prawns, from Dover Sole to eels, all arranged with infinite care by the men of Billingsgate to form a design of many shapes and colours. Fishermen's nets, draped at the back, bring a sense of salt sea air into the church. After the Service is over nothing is wasted, for Billingsgate donates this rich and varied catch to a charitable organization.

The Church of St Mary at Hill was built by Wren between 1670 and 1676 and is of exceptional beauty. The centre pews are reserved, very rightly, for the fish trade, but there is plenty of room in the side aisles for others who wish to attend, and all are welcome. The sermon, the lessons, the hymns – all are in thanksgiving for the harvest of the sea.

The Butterworth Charity – Distribution of Hot Cross Buns

Priory Church of St Bartholomew-the-Great, West Smithfield
(Good Friday – after the 11 am service)

This Good Friday custom originated in the seventeenth century, and has always consisted of a gift of hot cross buns and money to poor widows of the parish of St Bartholomew-the-Great, distributed from a flat tombstone in the churchyard. The Butterworth part of the title was introduced in the nineteenth century, when a Mr Joshua Butterworth bequeathed funds to ensure continuation of the charity in perpetuity. The choice of the same flat tombstone for the distribution has no particular meaning – merely that it is flat and suitable.

In 1973 no widow presented herself – for the first time in the history of the charity; so the Rector distributed the buns to the children of the congregation, who came forward very readily to collect the sticky hot cross buns from the dish lying on the tomb. Again, in 1974, the children enjoyed Mr Butterworth's Good Friday hot cross buns – and unless hard times and needy widows return to the parish this is the form that this delightful old custom is likely to take in the future.

The Spital Sermon

Church of St Lawrence Jewry Gresham Street (mid-May)

The custom of the Spital Sermon is of great antiquity. Its origin was the sermons on the Resurrection preached on the Monday, Tuesday and Wednesday of Easter from an open-air pulpit cross in the church-yard of the twelfth-century Priory Church of St Mary Spital, situated to the east of Bishopsgate (now Spitalfields). A spital was a place which received the poor and afflicted, and the Priory was divided between the brethren of the Order of St Augustine and lay members who tended the sick in the spital. From early times the Lord Mayor, Sheriffs and Aldermen attended the Spital Sermons, listening from a house of two storeys opposite the pulpit. The pulpit was destroyed in 1642, and after the Restoration of the Monarchy the sermons were preached in St Bride's Church, Fleet Street, and then in Christ's Church, Newgate Street. After war-time destruction of Christ's Church, St Lawrence Jewry became the final home of the annual Spital Sermon.

In the past the Spital Sermons were not only preached on the three days of Easter but were sometimes of great length. There is a record of Dr Barrow preaching a Spital Sermon which occupied three and a half hours; afterwards, when a weary member of the congregation asked if he were not tired, his reply was, 'Yes, indeed, I began to be weary with standing so long'. Today the Spital Sermon is represented by a service and sermon of average length. It is still attended by the Lord Mayor, Sheriffs and Aldermen, and is one of the occasions when the Lord Mayor attends in state – accompanied by his Household Escort of Swordbearer, Common Cryer and Serjeant-at-Arms, and the City Marshal. The Lord Mayor, with his Escort, walks to St Lawrence Jewry from the Aldermen's Court Room, off Guildhall Yard.

CHAPTER NINE

General

Some Theatrical Customs – old, and not-so-old

Twelfth Night used to be celebrated with masques, revels, and good-humoured jokes in which the natural order of things was reversed. Twelfth Night cakes were in great demand, and the pastrycooks of London did an enormous trade constructing vast cakes in elaborate forms. Now the custom has dwindled almost entirely – except for some instances in the world of the theatre.

The best known theatrical Twelfth Night cake in London is the Baddeley Cake at the Theatre Royal, Drury Lane, a custom unbroken (except for the war years) since the eighteenth century. The donor, Robert Baddeley (1732–1794) was one of the players at Drury Lane – but he had originally been a pastrycook and would, therefore, have deemed Twelfth Night an impossibility without a cake. It was while dressing for his part as Moses in Sheridan's *School for Scandal* that he fell ill and died, and in his will it was found that he had left £100 to provide annually for a Twelfth Night cake for the players at the Theatre Royal. His cake has been an occasion of celebration ever since.

Another theatrical cake which celebrates this night was inaugurated by Lilian Baylis in the 1920s and still continues in the world of Shakespeare, opera and ballet which she created as the Old Vic and Sadler's Wells and which has now emerged from its Vic-Wells chrysalis, spreading its wings as the fully fledged National Theatre, Royal Ballet, and English National Opera. The cake used to be cut alternately at the Old Vic and Sadler's Wells, and it used to be a real upside-down affair, with the singers dancing and the dancers singing, in the true spirit of Twelfth Night. Now, with the Old Vic and Sadler's Wells association sliding into oblivion, the partnership which launched so many world-famous names in drama, ballet and opera, perhaps this Twelfth Night cake may become known as the Lilian Baylis cake.

The Royal Ballet has its own end-of-season Taglioni cake, cut in the Green Room (beneath the stage) at the Royal Opera House, Covent Garden. Marie Taglioni (1809–84) occupies a special place in the history of ballet, for to her is attributed the introduction of dancing *sur les pointes*. In her later years she taught dancing and deportment to the children of our royal family, and she also took a few private pupils. One was a Miss Rolfe who, when herself an old lady, produced a collection of memoirs of Taglioni; among them appeared Taglioni's own recipe for her favourite cake. It is this cake which celebrates, each year, the end of the ballet season at Covent Garden (usually in July or August). In addition to the basic ingredients the cake contains quantities of walnuts, caraway seeds, rum, and 36 eggs. A distinguished ballet guest always cuts the cake.

The annual Grimaldi Commemoration Service presents a surprising scene on a Sunday afternoon in mid-March at Holy Trinity Church, Dalston, for this is the home church of the International Circus Clown Club, a number of whose members attend in full costume and make-up. It is a truly unusual procession which enters Holy Trinity Church for this service – with chalk-white faces, bright clown costumes, bulbous red noses and enormous clown's feet.

Joseph Grimaldi (1779–1837) was born in London of Italian descent – to a family of clowns and dancers; his father was Giuseppe Grimaldi, best known as Pantaloon in the Harlequinade. Joseph, who danced at Sadler's Wells at the age of three, was destined to become the greatest clown in English theatrical history. He created the clown character as we know it today, and he introduced the clown costume which has become traditional. His original costume is preserved in the London Museum.

The Grimaldi Commemoration Service is simple and gay, with emphasis throughout on the gift of laughter. The Clowns' Prayer is included, two clowns read the Lessons, and another lays a wreath on the simple Grimaldi memorial in the north-west corner of the church. The hymns, too, are bright and melodious, usually including the charming *Lord of the Dance*; and during the final hymn it has become the custom for each clown to receive a posy of fresh spring flowers gathered by the children of Tipton St John in Devon.

London's old-established dining clubs represent a subject far too voluminous to embark upon here, but there is one society so closely associated with the stage, and so long-lived, that I cannot resist mentioning it. This is the Sublime Society of Beef Steaks, founded in 1735 by John Rich, to whom is attributed creation of the pantomime in its uniquely English form. He was also creator of the English version of Harlequin. The Harlequinade had its origin in Italy and took many forms, but the rather romantic, graceful and silent figure, who dances with his Columbine and wears the traditional diamond-patterned costume, was the creation of John Rich. He himself appeared as Harlequin at Lincoln's Inn Fields, where he opened the theatre which his father, Christopher Rich (Manager of Drury Lane), had commenced building. Later John Rich built the Covent Garden Theatre, which he opened in 1733. His memory is kept green by the very restricted circle who form the membership of the Sublime Society of Beef Steaks – limited to 24 members, men only. Past membership has included some illustrious names, among them William Hogarth, Sir Henry Irving, Sir Johnston Forbes-Robertson, George Augustus Sala, Sir Lawrence Alma-Tadema, Sir Herbert Beerbohm Tree, John Wilkes (who adapted the Society's motto 'Beef and Liberty' for his election slogan 'Wilkes and Liberty'), and, most distinguished member of all, George IV when Prince of Wales.

Members of the Society meet monthly, and they hold a Grand Anniversary Dinner each January in commemoration of John Rich. Beef steak is, needless to say, the only meat served. Each member wears a Regency-style royal blue frock coat with buff waistcoat, and the President's head-dress is a Beefeater's hat (theatrical version). Another dignitary, 'the Bishop', wears a head-dress entitled Gregorio's Mitre, and 'The Recorder' wears Garrick's Hat, of three-cornered design and a replica of the original presented to the Society by David Garrick. Toasts include 'The Usual Toast' – 'Let none beyond this threshold bear away, what friend to friend in confidence may say', and the toast to Deceased Friends is accompanied by 'Fire', with the banging of glasses on the table.

Nearly two and a half centuries after its foundation by John Rich, this Society still meets – its jovial mood well-tuned to the pantomime which he created, but less so, one might say, to his other creation, the silent Harlequin.

Swearing on the Horns

The Wrestlers Inn, Highgate (an evening in Spring and Autumn)

Swearing on the Horns in Highgate is, and always has been, a 'joke' custom, but it used to be one in which most London-bound stage coach travellers from the north were expected to participate. A popular verse quoted in parts of the country far removed from Highgate shows how well known this rather odd bit of pantomime was:

> *It's a custom at Highgate that all who go through,*
> *Must be sworn on the horns, sir, and so, sir, must you.*

In 1826 there were 19 taverns in Highgate, and most of them kept a pair of horns for use in the 'ceremony' – some ram's horns, some stag's horns. As many as 80 stage coaches stopped per day at the Red Lion alone in the heyday of the stage coach, and three out of five travellers were usually sworn. As soon as the 'unsworn' travellers had been detected, the Landlord of the inn would don wig and black gown and then, accompanied by 'the Clerk', who carried a pole with the horns attached, the swearing would commence. When the era of the stage coach came to an end so, for a time, ended the custom of Swearing on the Horns; but early in the present century it was revived and, to the amusement of all, still continues on an evening in Spring and an evening in Autumn at the Wrestlers. 'The Judge' wears wig and black gown and, accompanied by the Clerk bearing the horns, administers the oath. The version used today (a version published in 1796) is as follows:

'Pray, Sir, lay your Right Hand on this Book, and attend to the Oath. You swear by the Rules of Sound Judgment that you will not eat Brown Bread when you can have white, except you like the Brown the better; that you will not drink Small Beer when you can get Strong, except you like the Small Beer better; but you will kiss the Maid in preference to the Mistress, if you like the Maid better – So help you Billy Bodkin – Turn around and fulfil your Oath'.

Following the Oath the candidate is declared a 'Freeman of Highgate', a privilege which has long been elucidated to the fortunate new 'Freeman' in the following vein:

'If at any time you are going through Highgate and want to rest yourself, and you see a pig lying in a ditch you have liberty to kick her out and take her place; but if you see three lying together you must only kick out the middle one and lie between the other two'.

The authorship of this inspired 'privilege' has been attributed to a local blacksmith who once kept the Coach and Horses Inn at Highgate and thought that he would add extra merriment to the proceedings.

In times past the custom of Swearing on the Horns obviously served as a good boost to trade at all the Highgate Inns. Today, at the Wrestlers, a certificate is given and a small charge made, the funds raised being donated to a local charity. It is all good fun, and long may it last.

Two East-End Customs Threatened by Change

At Fern Street and Devons Road, in Bromley-by-Bow, two customs linger on tenuously, for demolition plans could administer a death blow. Both are in areas suffering from pre-demolition blight, but at the time of writing they survive, which is ample excuse for including them.

The Farthing Bundles of Fern Street

This custom is not, in fact, very old, but it is an exceptionally charming one. It dates from 1907 when Miss Clara Grant founded the Fern Street Settlement in Bromley-by-Bow. Her aim was to bring help and courage to families living in the poorest streets of this East End community, and the children were her first consideration. Toys were a luxury beyond reach, the total lack of which inspired her to start the Farthing Bundles for the children, appealing to her friends in poetic form for as many small oddments as they could contribute, as well as other much-needed gifts. Here are a couple of her verses:

> *'Tis not for costly things we plead,*
> *Don't be alarmed, dear friends,*
> *For many things which give us joy*
> *Are just the 'odds and ends'.*
>
> *With us there's little comes amiss*
> *For nearly all is used,*
> *Either in keeping folks at work*
> *Or keeping them amused.*

Odds and ends poured in, and each child received a 'bundle', wrapped with newspaper and string; the packages were piled in bins on the pavement of Fern Street each Saturday morning – for sale; the payment was one farthing, the smallest coin of the realm. Miss Grant believed firmly that the children gained a sense of value, pride and independence from this tiny payment. So the Saturday morning Farthing Bundles came into being, and as time went by Miss Grant became known in Bromley-by-Bow as 'the Bundle Lady'.

One of the rules of the Farthing Bundle distributions was, and still is, that each child must be small enough to pass, without bending, beneath a wooden arch bearing the words:

> *Enter all ye children small,*
> *None can come who are too tall.*

This rule represented a necessary limitation of numbers, for in the early days of the Farthing Bundles up to 500 children would gather from 6 am onwards.

After Miss Grant's death the Settlement carried on with the same dedication as in the founder's lifetime. The Farthing Bundles are now distributed on alternate Saturdays, and the time is 8.45 am. The charge is now ½p and still the smallest coin of the realm – but no one would dream of referring to 'Halfpenny Bundles'. The original wooden arch is still in use and its ruling as firmly administered as ever. With changing times, however, and a more floating population the numbers of children are much smaller, and they tend to appear in a cluster at 8.45 am, then in ones and twos for the the next hour. Today much of the Settlement's work is for the elderly of Bromley-by-Bow, and in Miss Grant's original premises meals-on-wheels are served daily to more than 30 old age pensioners, for many of whom this luncheon gathering is the only social contact of the day.

Fern Street, as I have already said, is scheduled for demolition, and a deadness has crept along the street which is the familiar sign of the approaching bulldozer. The Settlement will have new and up-to-date premises, but there is sadness in the thought of the old rooms disappearing where such abundant kindness and help have always been offered. There is confidence, nevertheless, that the Farthing Bundles will continue, for they have become an East End tradition, and each time that the wooden arch appears on the Fern Street pavement the spirit of the Bundle Lady still seems to be very much alive in Bromley-by-Bow.

Hot Cross Buns at the Widow's Son Tavern
Devons Road, Bromley-by-Bow (Good Friday)

Only a few steps from Fern Street is the Widow's Son tavern in Devons Road, and like Fern Street it is in the path of the bulldozer. The demolishers have not yet reached the Widow's Son, however, and may not do so for a couple of years at least, so I will tell the tale of this curiously-named tavern. It has an unusual possession – a great cluster of mouldering buns, and it is the story of the buns that brings this East End pub into any narration of London's customs.

About 170 years ago this area presented a very different aspect from the poverty-stricken scene which Miss Grant encountered when she came to live there and founded the Fern Street Settlement in 1907. Here were meadows and country lanes, with rhubarb fields where Fern Street stands today; and on the site of the present-day tavern in Devons Road there was a cottage occupied by a widow. She had an only son, a sailor. One Easter, expecting him home, she bought hot cross buns on Good Friday and put one aside for him.

But he never came, that Easter or any subsequent Easter. No news of his death was received, and the widow, refusing to despair, kept the buns and added a new one each Good Friday to the cluster hanging from a beam in her cottage. After her death the cottage became known as the Bun House, and each Good Friday another hot cross bun was faithfully added. Eventually this cottage was demolished, and the present tavern was built on its site. The buns were still preserved and added to, and the pub was named the Widow's Son.

These venerable buns and their successors still hang from the bar ceiling of the demolition-condemned tavern. Occasional extra buns were added to mark special occasions – such as, for instance, the bun which commemorated Mafeking Night, and the one for the coronation of Queen Elizabeth II in 1953. Each Good Friday a stickily new hot cross bun joins the collection, and appropriately it is always a sailor who adds the new bun to the formidable mass of blackened dough which hangs from the ceiling.

Demolition is sometimes a ruthless but necessary process. Is it necessary, however, for the bulldozer to smash everything in its path, when restoration and a coat of paint would lend variation and a pocket of character among the new buildings? It is not only houses of great antiquity and beauty that merit preservation; so also do humbler buildings with no architectural claims yet harbouring a local tale of humanity. Soon very little of the past of Bromley-by-Bow will remain standing, and it would be an imaginative step to renovate and retain these two reminders of past life in the area – the three Fern Street houses where the Bundle Lady carried on her good work, and the neighbouring tavern where the buns of the lonely widow have been preserved for so long.

Index